THE JOURNEY BEGINS

Full Circle

Learning
to Live with Heart
and Purpose

LARRY HOLMES
with **PAUL KRON**

Full Circle: Learning to Live with Heart and Purpose
by Larry Holmes with Paul Kron

Published by: Nicasio Press,
                 Sebastopol, California
                 www.nicasiopress.com
Cover design: Constance King Design

ISBN: 979-8-9897756-6-8

For Mom and Dad,
Liler V. Holmes and Alfred "Freddie" Holmes

CONTENTS

Foreword i

Introduction 1

  1. Greetings from Neptune 5

  2. Lights on the Journey 27

  3. That Don't Make No Kinda Sense! 55

  4. We Will Take Care of Our Own 81

  5. Take the Controls! 99

  6. Defying Gravity 127

  7. Forks in the Road 141

  8. A Complete Game Changer 173

  9. Possibilities 191

  10. When the Student is Ready 211

Afterword 223

Acknowledgements 231

About the Author 233

FOREWORD

In this extraordinary "memoir with a purpose," Larry Holmes shares revealing and insightful stories of his circuitous journey into adulthood.

With candor and humility, he offers us hard-won insights into some of life's biggest challenges—how to recognize and overcome the mental shackles of race, religion, and politics; how to find inner freedom and peace; how to reach beyond the gravitational pull of limiting circumstances; how to find a deeper sense of purpose and meaning in our lives—to name a few.

With wit and wisdom, Larry demonstrates how our search for inner truth requires change and growth. Through example, he invites us to consider a deeper set of questions about who we are, why we're here, and how we might live into a broader set of possibilities. With kindness and empathy, he shows us how awareness and clear intentions are key to finding a greater sense of wholeness and unity. With compassion, he encourages us to more fully engage in our day-to-day lives, while remaining true to ourselves.

With grace—as one dear friend does for another— Larry's stories encourage us to reflect on our own unique life journey and invite us to sort out a few more of the answers for ourselves. They bring us light for the road up ahead and invite us to share it with others.

Bon Voyage.
Paul Kron
North Carolina

INTRODUCTION

WHAT'S YOUR STORY, MORNING GLORY?

"We tell our stories because all of us have survived something, because stories are signposts from the past that give us clues about the future...our stories are a witness to the next generation and an opportunity to understand the universal as well as the particular in tales of trauma, healing, and survival."
Barbara A. Holmes
Crisis Contemplation: Healing the Wounded Village

Life is a journey, whether we know it or not. Our stories are the signposts to help us gain clarity and make sense of the journey. This book is about the immense value of paying close attention to our life stories so we can begin to uncover the wisdom and insights they offer us.

As youngsters, if we looked out of sorts or confused, Mom would ask with a smile, "What's your story, morning glory?" The wisdom in her words was a gentle nudge to consider the internal narrative shaping our momentary perception of life. Little did I know how this everyday pearl of wisdom would come to define the nature and experience of my journey.

Dad, on the other hand, with his more serious demeanor, was more likely to shout his version of wisdom, "You better get moving, there's work to be done!" Two very different styles of teaching, but in a curious way, somehow pointing us in the same general direction. Though this was not always apparent to my young self.

Just a mile from the ocean on the Jersey shore, Neptune was on the other side of the tracks. Life's apparent limitations seemed to follow us like a shadow and suggest, "You won't amount to much. Why even try?" Some days, though, the ancient aroma of ocean air filled our little African American community and whispered a deeper truth in our hearts, "You are already someone. The possibilities are endless." This simple and genuine impulse called to me. Perhaps you've heard your version of it too?

I was quite shy as a kid, though I grew up in a loud and predominantly extroverted family. My mother joined me in my quietude, and it was often easy, if not always true, to feel unheard. When my schoolwork, basketball practice, or neighborhood explorations came to an end, I often retreated to the solitude of my room. Here, a private world of fantasy and heroics was on offer, full of exciting adventures, the righting of wrongs, and the prospect of exploring the world and having a positive influence, even making it a better place.

Given the racial, sporting, economic, and political circumstances of those days, these were bold dreams. Still, in those quiet hours, my whole and true self enjoyed a safe place. No matter the outside world, with its "Whites Only" signs, bent on keeping me contracted. Black kids like me were not welcome in most schools and colleges in those days, and I wondered if there even was a place for someone like me in a culture like this. Still, the prophetic words of Martin Luther King Jr. fed my soul with the prospects of hope, reconciliation, and the fulfillment of my emerging dreams. "Why not?" I thought. Even if it was small, I could play some part in bringing people together despite our differences. Such intentions lay deep inside each of us, and I imagined summoning the courage to bring these dreams to the light of day. The journey ahead would be long and circuitous.

This book is a collection of stories about some of the most challenging and transformative experiences in my transition from childhood into early-adulthood. These stories chronicle many of the experiences that led to my study and practice of—and deep passion for—Western developmental psychology and Eastern philosophy and meditation practices. My integration of these approaches and worldviews, ultimately became the springboard for much of the transformational leadership and organizational work I've been involved with over the past forty years.

Filtered through decades of time, these stories are sketched from distant memories, and informed by the cultural, economic, and political dissonance that awoke my generation during the 1950s, 60s, and 70s. They are stories that serve as reminders of how personal tendencies and external circumstances so often squelch our resolve and inhibit our best intentions. They also demonstrate the immense value of receiving light and encouragement from others to help us keep moving through or around whatever seemingly insurmountable obstacles we encounter along our way.

This book, then, brings me full circle as an expression of my deep gratitude to the countless wise and loving people who've come to my aid and so generously provided their particular form of light. In that spirit, I offer my version of the story, not as one who has completed the journey or learned all the lessons, but as a fellow traveler who has encountered some universal signposts worth sharing. Consider it an invitation for you to curate and mine your own unique life stories, and in profound new ways, discover and celebrate the richness of this amazing thing we call "life."

With my whole heart, I invite you, both in real time and through the luxurious gift of hindsight, to search out the priceless stories and embedded wisdom life is so patiently and lovingly eager to teach us about the purpose of our journey.

With much love and deep respect,
Larry Holmes
Neptune, New Jersey

1

GREETINGS FROM NEPTUNE

In the shadow of the city and on the doorstep of the Atlantic Ocean, life was good.

New York City was the center of our universe. As kids, my friends and I figured if you had the good fortune to live in or even just near "The City," as we did, you had it made. The population of our little town of Neptune ebbed and flowed with the seasons. But the "city that never sleeps" was just a quick drive away, and we felt connected to the whole world. With Philadelphia and D.C. to our south, and Newark and Boston just a few hours north, this was where it was all happening, and we could feel it in our bones.

East of Neptune, on the Jersey shore, the popular beachside town of Asbury Park and surrounding area played above itself in producing well-known personalities like Jack Nicholson, Jon Bon Jovi, Danny DeVito, and the great Count Basie. Bruce Springsteen was in school in nearby Freehold when I was in school in Neptune. He played in the clubs along the shore and did free gigs at the Stone Pony across from the boardwalk. The name of his first album came from a popular postcard—*Greetings from Asbury Park.*

Located just a mile from the ocean, summers in Neptune were all about spending time at the beach and exploring the delights of the boardwalk: The ever-changing cast of characters. The rides that made us dizzy. The jumble of tunes filling the salty air. The aroma of fried food and cotton candy teasing our taste buds. The wild dance of colors and curvaceous figures at the Easter Sunday Fashion Parade. Each summer, the shore promised a new adventure of magic and delight.

Neptune was a quiet town for most of the year. The streets of our neighborhood were our playground and ball field. The little woods behind our house invited us to build tree houses and forts. We roamed unencumbered and morphed magically into wild animals, intrepid explorers, and brave soldiers fighting for freedom. The possibilities were endless. Watching the stars at the end of the day, there was also a sense of more beyond this safe little harbor, and I felt deeply drawn to it. Where, I wondered, did all this come from? Why were we here? And what would it take to explore the wider world beyond this place I called home?

Outside our neighborhood we knew there were plenty of limits. And we knew it wasn't right. Most folks in Neptune and Asbury Park were white. The area where we lived was one of the few lower-class, black neighborhoods.

Our first house was at 13½ First Street. People always asked, "A half?" That half, though, was deeply symbolic for me, as a reminder of how I felt treated at times—like less than a full citizen.

The elementary school in our neighborhood was just a block and a half away. All the students were black, except for four white kids. Racial segregation and the inequalities it fostered were the norm, simply a part of the landscape.

In high school civics class, we learned about the *Brown versus Board of Education* Supreme Court decision ruling that "separate-but-equal" is not, in fact, equal, and segregation in public schools is unconstitutional. But it didn't change our lives in Neptune. Regardless of what some court decided, most black people in the 1950s and 1960s felt they were going to be subjected to discrimination, and four hundred years of slavery in the Americas had taught us that rocking the boat was dangerous. From the point of view of building an egalitarian society, racial segregation was clearly not a good thing. But in many ways, our neighborhood and school were sheltered. And as a shy, young, black boy, it seemed to make my life a bit simpler, and perhaps less stressful.

I wouldn't say we had a lot of money. We didn't. But our small and simple home on First Street was clean, and we had all the basics, in my estimation. Just inside the side entrance of our house was a little space for storing hats, mittens, and snow boots, and to hang heavy winter coats. This led into a slightly larger sitting area. On particularly cold days, Mom would stoke up the coal-burning stove and open up its little door to coax the hand-washed laundry to dry. On one side of the sitting room was a doorway leading to the kitchen, which is where we spent a majority of our time together as a family. In one corner was a Formica-topped table just big enough to accommodate four chrome chairs, with bright red vinyl seats. In the other corner was a narrow set of steeply ascending stairs leading to our three modest bedrooms and a small bathroom upstairs. Our living room was at the front of the house and held our family's "good furniture"—which was strictly reserved for special occasions and guests. No part of our little abode was spacious, but I always liked it. It felt just right to me.

We had more than most of the families in our neighborhood. It was strange to live in a poor area but not feel the impact of poverty in the same way we knew others did. Mom and Dad owned their own home and had a nice car—two actually. And as a successful chef, Dad often brought good food home from work. There was never a feeling of being deprived, and the depth and breadth of economic inequities that came with being a black kid in America were mostly lost on me.

Single-parent families were common in our neighborhood. Mothers were most often the head of their household and dads were often not around. Our area was considered rough, tough, and dangerous. *Life Magazine* named Springwood Avenue, our town's main drag, "one of the ten most dangerous streets in America." I didn't hang out there, but my barber shop was there, and I felt comfortable with that.

During those early years, friends were getting into trouble. Drugs, drink, and violence meant some didn't make it out of high school or survive for long afterwards. More than enough died young, and our folks kept a close eye on our whereabouts and the company we kept. It felt overly cautious and annoyingly restrictive, but it might well be why we're still around to tell the tale.

Mom and Dad grew up under the heavy weight of the Deep South's Jim Crow segregation laws, and the heartache and struggles those unjust laws spawned. That's why they left. In 1942, within a few months of taking their marriage vows, they packed up their few possessions and moved sight unseen to make a fresh start in Neptune. Dad told Mom,

"I got a good job cooking up north in New Jersey, at a big hotel near the ocean."

Mom didn't like the thought of moving away from home.

"My family is all here, Freddy," she implored. "And it's just too cold up there."

But Dad insisted, "Lil, I'm not even gonna think about raising no family down here. It just ain't gonna happen!" And that, as they say, was that. The move was made, but "home" came with them.

It's not that Dad thought the North was without its problems, of all shapes and sizes. But he was adamant his future family was going to have a better beginning than he and Mom had. They were both raised in single-parent families. When they were in their mid-teens, the Great Depression was in full swing, and living with little or nothing was the norm. The black shantytowns of rural Florida made for a difficult childhood for both of them.

Mom wanted the same but was a bit less outspoken about it. When she told us about that time, she said she resolved to herself, "I'll create my family environment up North then." She embraced the adventure with her usual grace and charity.

From time to time, we went back to visit Mom's mother, Allie May, and our great-grandmother, Anna Griffin, in Lynn Haven, Florida. We were always amazed by how hot it was there. We sipped sweet iced tea on the front porches of their little homes, which to me and my sister, Pat, weren't much more than shacks. We found out later that their homes were originally slave quarters, and that our great-grandmother's mother had been one of the many slaves in Lynn Haven.

When no one was looking, we made astonished faces at each other because the water smelled and tasted like sulfur, which, to us kids meant "bad." And when we asked to use the bathroom, to our great surprise, we were pointed outside. "Out back, hon'," Gramma Mack grinned and pointed. "The outhouse is just out back." We opened the creaky wooden door to study the unfamiliar setup. A swarm of flies and an astonishingly strong odor met our open mouths.

This was my first exposure to full-on, in-your-face poverty and racial segregation, and along with the "Whites Only" signs at eating places and gas stations, it felt unfair and overwhelmingly demeaning.

I really don't like it down here, I thought to myself on the long drive home. When I get old enough, I'm not coming down here for these visits. I'm staying home.

I was torn though. I felt a great affection for my grandmother and great-grandmother, who welcomed us into their modest homes with such love.

But this just isn't right, my young mind objected, to treat us this way. It makes me feel bad to see or even think about members of my family being treated like this. Are we really not good enough?

As a young boy, Dad told himself, "When I make good, I'm gonna help Mama get outta that place." But she died quite young, and it was always a great disappointment to him. He loved her deeply.

Dad was born in 1917. He told us stories about the harsh conditions of growing up poor in the South, but not in a complaining kind of way.

"I'm mostly just lucky to be alive," he'd start. "I went out one night riding in a car with a group of boys. There weren't any streetlights or guardrails back then, and the boy driving was just fifteen. He lost control. The car went over the side of a rickety old wooden bridge, and we all dropped down into the river and out of sight. It was cold and dark, and I was pretty sure I was a goner. In fact, two of my friends got stuck and drowned inside that car. I got stuck too, plus I had a big ole' gash in my thigh and lots of blood was coming out of it. The boy who was driving pulled me out. He saved my life.

"But I was hurt pretty bad. The ambulance came, but to them, we were just black boys, and they didn't pay too much mind to how they treated us. They sewed me up like an old rag. It's never been right since. That's just how it was back then."

The scar on Dad's thigh always looked like a chunk of muscle was missing. He struggled a lot with that leg in his later years. But he didn't complain. His stories made us feel fortunate to be growing up where and when we did. And grateful too, for the courage Mom and Dad had to make a better life for themselves and us children.

The other families on First Street were a mixed bag. Our next-door neighbors were Hispanic. With five young children running around, it was never clear how they all fit into their small but impeccably clean home. The family's father had a steady job as a cook and was seldom seen. Their mother was a big woman, who ruled with a loving but unwaveringly firm hand. Her rapid-fire Spanish was often heard in concert with swift punishments for the slightest hints of misbehavior from her children. At suppertime, her booming voice shouted out orders and warnings over the intoxicating aromas of her Mexican cooking, which wafted around the neighborhood. The kids were all very well behaved and took the teasing they received for their broken English in stride. Life didn't seem easy for them, but they were good students and good athletes too. They were always polite and nice to everyone. They smiled a lot.

Next to the family from Mexico was an African American family of hard-to-determine numbers. Their house was a rambling kind of structure, and day and night, a wide variety of people seemed to always be coming and going. It was hard to tell who lived there and who didn't. It also wasn't clear what the parents did for a living. They had a good-sized front porch that was always filled with people and loud conversations. It was fun to watch and sometimes to participate. Two of the five kids who appeared to live there became our friends, and though they were older and considerably bigger than me, we often played together. In the field behind our houses, we imagined ourselves to be soldiers.

"I shot you—you're dead."

"What? No way. I shot you first, you're already dead."

Sometimes we were explorers and built forts out of branches for our survival. We climbed trees and dared one another to venture higher. In the summer, we played stickball in the street.

"That's a home run."

"Uh uh, it's a foul ball."

"No way—home run."

Similar conversations occurred while playing football in the fall.

"That's a touchdown."

"What? My finger touched your pants. You're down." Arguing was an essential part of every game.

We grew apart when we entered high school. College preparatory classes and basketball became my focus, and they hung out with a different, older crowd. Also, all the families on First Street had to move out because our homes had to be sold and demolished to make way for low-cost, public housing.

Mom and Dad considered other places for building our new home.

"There's larger blocks of land in other townships," they suggested. "We'd get more land for less money, and you kids could still be pretty close to our old neighborhood. What do you think?"

It would be hard to leave our friends and familiar surroundings, and there was no knowing what another school and a new group of students would be like for us.

"Nope," we answered in practiced unison, "we're good staying here in Neptune and close to our friends."

It was exciting moving into a new house. It was also a little sad to be leaving our old neighborhood. As basic as it was, it was home for us. We told ourselves, "We'll still be less than a mile from our friends, right? Plus, we'll be going to the same high school." In reality, our lives changed quite a bit from that point onwards. My parents eventually lived in that new house of ours by Sand Hill for forty-five years.

There were four kids and two cousins in our family. Alfred Junior was the oldest. He was born to a different mother down south before Mom and Dad were married. When Dad and Mom moved north, it created a question about where Junior would live. The initial arrangement was for him to spend a school year with his mother down south, and then spend a school year with his dad up north in Neptune. It was a good plan on paper. But we didn't hear much from anyone down south for quite a long while, and one day Dad announced, "I think I'll just go down and visit some of my relatives in Florida." We all knew the reason for his trip. He was worried, and Dad preferred action to worry.

He drove down to see how things were going and was shocked to discover Junior wasn't in school. He was working the cotton fields in torn, ragged clothes and bare feet. Dad was angry, and then and there, the living arrangements changed. From then on, Junior lived with us full time. "He ain't never going back down to that place. That ain't never gonna happen!" Dad proclaimed. We didn't think of him as a stepbrother. He was just our brother. Simple as that.

Mom and Dad expected Junior to lead the way and set the example for the rest of us. When we were youngsters, he was playfully but quite persistently fond of teasing us. Our sister, Pat, was nine years younger than Junior, and I came along a year and a day after her. We thought of ourselves as twins.

Ralph came ten years after us. He and Dad had similar interests and spent a lot of time together. After Pat got married and moved out, and I went off to college, Ralph and Dad got to know each other well.

Our cousins Victor and Bruce spent a lot of time at our house. Their parents—Mom's baby sister, Johnnie Mae, and her husband, Purcell—both died young. So, they were always considered a part of our family. We loved each other and felt very close. That's how family was for us.

Mom's given name was Liler, but most everyone called her Lil. She was a natural-born caregiver and home builder and created the steady heart of quiet love in our family. Dad provided the structure and rules. Mom was all sweetness and forgiveness—unless you broke the rules. Her nickname was, in fact, "Honey," and people simply wanted to be around her. Dad was particular about the kind of people he wanted around. Mom, on the other hand, was always keen to make everyone feel welcome.

As various relatives moved up from the South, Mom would quietly inform us, "One of your cousins is coming to spend the summer with us. Please make her feel comfortable." These visits provided a glimpse into the life our parents were building for us. We would hear our guests say, "Freddie, this is some home you got here. I wonder if we could get a place like this? Could you all help us find a place to stay maybe?" In this way, we slowly but surely became a large extended family. Soon enough we had uncles, aunties, and cousins in our neighborhood or nearby along the Shore. It was like a warm and comforting circle of extended family.

Part of our tradition was that family members and close friends dropped by our house on a regular basis. There was no formality about it. Just a knock on the door at any hour, and they would come on in.

"Hey there. Anybody home?"

Most times they didn't wait for an answer.

"What you got cooking, Lil?"

When black friends came to our house complaining about white people, Mom didn't say much. But we all understood she didn't like hearing anyone say something bad about another person, regardless of their color or culture. Her life-long practice was to be kind in her words and actions, and whenever possible, uplift others.

When things were tough, Mom would say, "Don't ever feel sorry for yourself. You can make something of yourself. You just have to be strong and believe in yourself."

Her message was always the same:

"Love each other, depend on each other, stay tight, and don't just hate those who look different from you. There are all sorts of people in God's kingdom. Remember, it's up to us to find out who the good ones are."

She was kind to everyone and didn't have a bad word about anyone. If someone tried to draw her into criticizing another person, she quietly mouthed, "Hmm," and otherwise stayed silent. Applying Mom's approach to our own interactions was a challenge, though her unwavering example was always there as an encouragement.

Mom was a great cook. Her specialty was southern fried chicken, and everyone loved it. On Sundays, we went to church and afterwards, she would fry up a batch of chicken she'd marinated in her own special mixture of spices overnight. She spent most Sunday afternoons in the kitchen as people came and went.

"Hey, Lil, you got some more of your chicken? Got any rice or sweet potatoes, Honey? Oh, and how 'bout some collard greens or okra if you got 'em?"

Cooking for her family and friends was a labor of love for Mom, and her kitchen door was always open. Once I asked,

"Mom, how do you make your food taste so good?"

"Well," she reflected, "you can't just fry chicken any ole' way and expect it to taste like mine. You gotta pay attention to all the details. And you have to do it all with love."

When I hung out with Mom in her kitchen, she wanted to know all about what was happening in my life.

"How are you doing with your studies? Not that I could help much, we didn't even finish grammar school. And how about your sports? Are you enjoying your basketball? Did you know I played basketball in school too?"

"Really? I never knew that, Mom," I said. "Did you like it?"

"Oh yes, I did like it. Back then it was called girls' basketball and the rules were different. There were six girls on each team. I was short, but I could shoot." This was about the most bragging you would hear from our mom.

For Mom, home and family life were most about attitude and feeling. Rules and responsibilities were Dad's forte. But if you broke the rules that kept us safe, Mom would let you know by showing her mostly hidden, fierce side. Once, while Dad was away with work, my sister, Pat, and I ventured to the end of our one-block street to the house of an older boy. We lost track of time and stayed past our curfew. Suddenly, we heard someone pounding on the door. When our friend opened the door, there was Mom with fire in her eyes. She ignored him and came straight for us.

"I told you never to come up here." she yelled, and started giving us a whipping with a switch she'd brought with her just for the occasion. "Don't you ever come up here again." And we surely never did.

Dad tended to have a distinct view of what was right and what was wrong. In fact, he had an opinion about most everything. He jumped into any conversation on any subject floating around the house. Letting things drift or go unchallenged, especially if something differed from his perspective, was extremely unlikely. If we complained about one another, he was quick to point out,

"Now, families can be their own worst enemies. Your family is all you got. You need to be grateful for them, and love and protect each other. I get so angry if I see my children arguing or fighting with each other. You already got other people trying to tear you down, and now you gonna tear yourselves apart? That don't make no kind of sense. And it don't take no degree to know that."

That was one of Dad's favorite put-downs. Sometimes I felt uncomfortable with the way he expressed his opinions. Like there was no other way to look at or express things. But, I thought, at least he's not talking about me.

He never stopped preaching from his particular philosophy for living. Another one of his constant messages was,

"Family is what you can depend on when things get tough. You should love your brothers and your sisters. If you teach your children the importance of family as they grow up, if you show them how to treat each other right, and to respect their parents, then good things will happen in your family." Dad didn't have a strong and intact family structure growing up and he clearly didn't want us to take such a gift for granted.

Some in our extended family tended to speak off the top of their head, without really thinking it all the way through. "The problem is the people with all the money and power just want to keep us black folks poor and not let us succeed. Just like down south, all they wanna do is keep us in the outhouse."

Dad started grinding his teeth and shaking his head to such claims, and without skipping a beat, he pointed a stiff finger at the speaker, and retorted with,

"Now that's just dumb. If you don't know what you talkin' about, don't say nothing, cause you just sound stupid, and now people know you're stupid." Then he'd have a good chuckle, adding, "Ain't no one can really keep you down if you set your mind on a goal and go after it with all your heart. It don't do no good blaming others for keeping you down. You just gotta get up and keep moving forward. That's the honest truth." Quietly, I wondered if that was really possible in this world that seemed set on keeping people like us down.

When someone mentioned a person Dad felt to be stubbornly wrong, he'd say, "He ain't got no sense. Don't listen to him. He ain't worth a quarter." And one of his all-time favorite jabs as roving judge, jury, and prosecutor was, "Case closed. Guilty as charged."

With few exceptions, to my mind, Mom remained the model of patience and kindness, combined with both inner and outer strength. On the other hand, Dad's style was more in your face. Along with his tightly-held points of view, he maintained a swift and decisive temper. And as a professional chef running a loud and bustling kitchen, the tenor of his voice tended toward loud and commanding.

For a black man coming from a highly segregated and racially abusive environment down south, Dad had a surprising take on the topic of racial discrimination.

"I'll tell you what," he'd say. "Black people can do more harm to each other than what white people can do, 'cause white people aren't there with you all the time. Some of the worst people I know are black. And some of the nicest people I know are white. Black people don't wanna hear me saying that, but it's the truth. It ain't got nothing to do with the color of your skin. It's the people. And each person is different, black or white. Don't forget that." When questioned on this, he told a story about growing up in the South.

"Me and my friends were driving around one night, late. We got lost and found ourselves in a fancy, white neighborhood. We got all turned around and then we ran out of gas. We didn't exactly know where we were really. But we did know for sure, we weren't supposed to be there. We were all thinking that this is exactly the kind of place where bad things happen to folks who look like us.

"We didn't know what to do. Even getting out of the car seemed dangerous. And then, wouldn't you know, a bunch of white boys came walking on by and saw us, and the situation we were in. They were poking each other, and one of the bigger kids started walking straight toward us with a mean-looking grin on his face. We braced ourselves for some kind of trouble. And then a car pulled up behind us with their lights shining right into the back window of our car. We were all thinking, 'Now this is really getting bad!'

"Their doors all swung open, and a second, bigger group of white guys got out. The one driving came right over to us and said as friendly as could be, 'Hey, you fellas having troubles with your car? You need some help, maybe? How 'bout we drive you where you need to be?'"

"And you know what?" Dad asked, with a catch in his throat. "You can be sure we were grateful for their kindness. So, you see, you just can't say a whole race is bad or good. It depends. Don't judge too quickly is all."

"We want you children to know that your friends are always welcome here in our home. Invite them to come see you here." This was the reassuring mantra we heard consistently from both Mom and Dad when we were coming along. It was good to know we were encouraged to bring our friends home. Later, we caught on that it was also a clever way of checking out our companions.

"If you hang out with the wrong people you get caught in their web." This was another of Dad's common themes. "I've seen it a hundred times. Choose your friends wisely, is all." Among the young people in our area, there were a few, like that boy up the street, who could be called "the wrong kind of friends." It wasn't that they were mean or bad, certainly not to us.

Though their styles were quite different, Dad and Mom loved us dearly. Each in their own way. Dad fiercely, Mom sweetly. Neither of them had the opportunity as kids to finish grammar school. Working to help support their families at an early age was more important. Consequently, the importance of education and learning was another perpetual topic in our home.

"You kids have got to study hard and get a college education. That's the only way you have a chance of getting ahead in this world." This was the ever-present drumbeat of our young lives, and regardless of how often we rolled our eyes or felt the pressure of unrelenting expectations, it did not stop.

Dad had learnt mainly from watching and listening, especially at work, not from going to school. It was the same for Mom. They both made their way with natural smarts and courage.

"I really feel like if I had an education, I could have done anything," Dad said to our younger brother, Ralph, one Sunday afternoon.

"Dad," Ralph responded incredulously, "I think you're missing something. Look at where you've come from and what you were able to do for all of us without an education."

Dad reflected for a bit.

"Yeah, I think you're right, son. I never thought about it like that."

Before Dad was able to find higher paying, year-round work, Mom did housework for white families. This bothered Dad to no end, and as youngsters we often overheard them arguing about it.

"Lil," Dad would start in, "I don't like you having to do that kind of work. That's why we came up north, so you wouldn't have to clean other people's houses. We can find you something better."

"Well, yes," she answered quietly. "But we can use the money right now, Freddie, and I don't mind doing it." She really didn't mind. We knew she was doing it out of love for her family and with her head held high.

Slowly, Mom was able to get more of what Dad called "dignified work." She became a school-crossing guard at our primary school. Later, she got work at the township library, where she stayed until she retired. Over the years, she would pull me aside and quietly ask,

"Can you help me with my letters for reading, son? I have to be better at it for this job." Or she'd say, "Larry, honey, I need to be better with my numbers. Can you help me?"

Her humble and simple requests for help revealed deep feelings of love and sadness inside me and led me to marvel at her inner strength.

"Sure, Mom, show me what you're working on."

Dad didn't go to any culinary school to become a chef. That wasn't likely to happen for a black man growing up in the South in the 1930s and 1940s. As a kid in the midst of the Great Depression, he noticed that one of his uncles always had nice clothes, a car, and some walkin'-around money in his pocket.

"What does Uncle do?" he asked his mom.

"He cooks."

Dad immediately responded, "But you cook and we don't have nothin'."

His mom just smiled. "You know those big hotels downtown, owned by the rich white folks? Well, he cooks in those places."

According to Dad, "Right then and there, I made up my mind that I was going to become a cook. The big question was how was I going to make that happen?

"Each day, I took a few of my friends, and we went down to the back of one of those big hotels and played in the back alley where they put out the garbage and all. One day, a man who looked important came out.

"He looked at me and said, 'You boy, you want a job?'

"Yes sir, I do," I said.

"And that's how I got started. I worked my way up. I knew it was going to be a long, hard road to my goal. I started out as a dishwasher and general kitchen hand. But I also started studying cookbooks in my free time. Eventually, I got the courage to share some of my ideas with the cooks."

"What happened then?" I asked Dad.

"Well," he said, "cooks, especially chefs, don't like you telling them what they should do. So, I lost a few jobs."

Looking back on those early days with the perspective of how life eventually turned out for him, he laughed as he told me this story.

"And then one of the chef's did listen to what I had to offer. This one chef said, 'Okay, you work with me.' That was the road to how I became a chef."

Dad was also a good musician. He played the trombone and at one time even had his own small band. He was good, too. I especially remember how good he sounded when he practiced at home. Loud, but good. And when he played "Danny Boy," it was so smooth and sweet that it almost brought tears to my eyes. Maybe it was then that I sensed there were more sides to Dad than met the eye. He gave up the band to give his full attention to raising our family. What a sacrifice that must have been for him. He loved his music. His love of music was contagious enough to lure me into playing the trombone too. I picked up his love of music at an early age.

My first job was working with Dad, when he was the head chef in a big hotel restaurant down on the Shore in Long Branch, called "Miss Yvonne's." It was a weekend job that he would do sometimes to supplement his regular income. He got me a job as a dishwasher, the same first job he had as a kid. Dad stressed that I had to work hard and fast. He was an uncompromising taskmaster. One night I had quickly finished off the first round of pots and dishes and was waiting for the next rush. I was casually standing by the sink with my hands in my pockets.

"What are you doing? Get your hands out of your pockets!" my dad yelled at me. "Don't you ever put your hands in your pockets in this place. There's too much work to be done!"

It was embarrassing as the rest of the kitchen staff were all watching and listening. It felt like they were probably laughing at me on the inside. It also felt like Dad was being overly strict because I was his son. It was one of those incidents when, as a young person, I felt like I was being treated unfairly, and Dad's in-your-face way of doing things upset me.

The next weekend, during a busy time in the kitchen, one of the other cooks yelled at me, "Hey, boy, come over here and take these pots away."

My dad was busy preparing meals to be served but suddenly stopped.

"What did you call him?"

The cook obviously sensed he had said something wrong and mumbled, "I just asked him to pick up these pots."

My dad went over to him, "No you didn't. You called him 'boy,' didn't you? Do you have a name?" he asked the cook.

"Yeah."

"Well, so does he." My dad was angry. "His name is Larry, not 'boy,' and you better call him that." Dad was heating up now.

As Dad was saying this, he was waving the knife he was preparing the meal with in his hand. It added even more tension to the situation.

He turned and went back to work, but he didn't let it go. He was like that. When he got hot, which was more than seldom, it would take a while for him to cool down. Every couple of minutes he would blurt out, in great disgust, to no one in particular, "Boy? His name isn't 'boy.' Is your name 'boy'?" Then he'd turn back to cooking.

In fact, throughout the entire incident, he never stopped cooking, preparing meals, yelling, "Up!" to the waiters and waitresses when each meal was ready. He was a study in total focus and continual motion. And he could carry on an entire conversation with himself while he did it.

Calling someone "boy" was akin to going back to the relationship and language of slave and master. Dad had left the South to get away from all of that. This was 1963, in New Jersey. What Dad did that night was eye-opening and uplifting for me. Possibly for the others in the kitchen too. He challenged the old ways, but at the same time, he kept doing his job in the most professional way. It wasn't easy to work in a kitchen with him, but I learned a lot, and not just about cooking. That night I also started to learn how important it is to feel confident and stand up for yourself, even in awkward situations.

Slowly, there were opportunities to learn actual cooking tasks like chopping and preparing vegetables and other ingredients for the different dishes. In those big kitchens, we were always feeding lots of people with huge quantities of everything. Kitchen hands like me had to peel fifty-pound bags of potatoes or onions at a time.

"Hey, Larry," one of the cooks would call out, "we need this bag of onions peeled for the soup we're preparing." It was all about staying focused, learning a skill, and moving on to the next thing to be done.

I didn't want to have a cooking career. For me, it was mainly a way to make some money and maybe learn a thing or two in the process. It was hard physical work and the long hours, weekends, and nights were not when I wanted to be working. To me, those were the times for living life.

Given the political, racial, and economic upheavals of the 1950s and 1960s, we had it pretty good. Especially if we didn't look too far outside of our neighborhood. We had a two-parent family and good friends. We owned our own home, had plenty to eat, and two cars to get around town in. Sure, there were some tensions, particularly when Mom and Dad had different approaches or points of view. But the differences seemed to be more about how to get to the same goals. Perhaps the biggest challenges for us kids were achieving good grades, staying out of trouble, and keeping work going to pay for our college education. Uncertainties were mainly about how us kids would eventually make our way in life.

In the shadow of the city and on the doorstep of the Atlantic Ocean, life was good. And yet, by the time high school was coming to an end, it was clear that my dream for the future was about seeing and experiencing the world beyond my little hometown.

2

LIGHTS ON THE JOURNEY

Martin Luther King Jr. was somehow able to be against the injustices of our society without being against the people perpetrating them. That struck me as being very true and very powerful... The inclusiveness of his language offered a compelling challenge and mandate to include and heal all of us in the great American dream. Yet another light in the darkness.

Like many young teenagers, sports—basketball for me—became my known and safe haven. It was potentially a way out of the limiting circumstances of the hood. It could also save my parents thousands of dollars in college fees if I got good enough. To be honest, it was also an acceptably legitimate way to get out of the house when, like most kids that age, I just needed to keep moving.

From sixth grade on, I became passionate about basketball. My driving force was simply the love of the game. My interest grew when I started watching games on TV with my older brother, Junior. He explained the finer points of the game and pointed out the great players, especially in the NBA.

"Elgin Baylor plays for the Lakers," Junior explained, "and is the most talented player in the league. He's only six feet, five inches tall but out-rebounds much taller players. He seems to float through the air…just hanging there until the defending players return to the floor. Then he releases his shot. Unbelievable athleticism."

Based on Junior's commentary, Baylor immediately became my favorite player. The powerful and fluid flow of his game and the way he combined his highly honed dribbling skills and acrobatic body movements to score baskets was amazing. His graceful movements around the court looked challenging but exciting and fun at the same time. That attracted me. It would be so much fun to do that. To just hang in the air like that—to defy gravity!

Like so many other young boys, I was hooked. As soon as the school day was over, one of my friends would say,

"Hey, let's play some ball after school."

"Yeah, that sounds great. Let's meet at Jake's house."

We came home from school, changed into our basketball clothes, and headed off to play in our friend's backyard. We'd play for hours. Even in the winter or when it got dark, we kept playing. One of us would say, "Hey, man, it's getting kinda dark to see the ball and the basket." Someone else would say, "No way, man, it's okay, my night vision radar is clicking in now. The real problem is it's getting too hard to see you, dude." Then we would crack up with laughter. We developed a kind of sixth sense to tell us where the basket and the ball was.

Even when it snowed, someone would still suggest, "Hey, let's play some ball, it's not so cold. The snow makes it feel a little warmer."

We cleared as much snow as possible, packed down what was left, and played on it. We came to know that backyard intimately. My hands would go numb, but gloves got in the way of the all-important "feel" for the ball. It didn't matter. We played on. We loved it. Without knowing it, we learned persistence and grit. In that space, we felt free. No boundaries. And freedom from boundaries, it seemed, was something I was looking for, without being aware of what it really was.

One funny thing about my love for basketball was that for the first thirteen years of my life, my parents, Mom in particular, imagined they had discouraged me from doing any strenuous exercise. I wasn't even aware of this until many years later when we were having a casual conversation and the topic of basketball came up.

"Of course, we were careful not to let you do very physical things when you were young because of your heart murmur," my mother said.

"Heart murmur? Mom, you never told me this."

She smiled her sweet smile. "Maybe we didn't, but I was always scared something might happen. That's why when you wanted to play basketball at school in eighth grade, we put you into the hospital to have a whole lot of tests."

I do remember the week I spent in hospital undergoing a whole battery of tests. It wasn't fun. Fortunately, the test results were all negative, in large part, because—according to my expert, the thirteen-year-old brain—I had already decided that nothing was going to stop me from playing basketball. I was relatively short as a basketball player, barely five foot, ten inches, and with a thin frame. There was also this feeling that, as one of the youngest in my class, I had to catch up to the other guys, who were generally older, taller, bigger, and stronger.

Our little, segregated elementary school and middle school were just around the corner from our house and neighborhood. Close, known, and comfortable. Most of our classmates lived in the same part of town and had been friends for years. Neptune High was newly built in 1960 to accommodate students from five primary school districts. The transition into an integrated high school felt swift and monumental. In a flash, we found ourselves in a sea of fifteen hundred strangers, and social, economic, and racial differences were suddenly up close and personal.

Mom sensed some weight on our shoulders. As we headed out the door in the morning, she asked, "How are you all feeling today? Do you have everything you need? I can drive you if you want."

"No thanks, Mom," we all answered. "We're walking with our friends."

My sister, Pat, walked and gossiped with her girlfriends. I walked with the guys and gossiped about different things. Mostly sports, girls, and racial tensions. Our mile-long walk up to Sand Hill felt long. Especially on icy, cold days. Wearing heavy winter coats, hats, and boots, we slowly trudged along, pulling our hats down over our ears, bending over to protect ourselves from the bitter wind. Sometimes we even walked backwards to shield our face and chests from the piercing cold.

"Jesus, help us, we're all going to freeze to death," someone would shout, and then we'd laugh and push ourselves forward. We cursed passing cars with classmates getting cozy rides to school. "Momma's boys," we moaned. We knew how to be strong, or at least appear that way. As we neared the crest of the hill, we watched the school buses arrive from the other, more well-to-do parts of the township. As the kids piled off into the cold, they smiled and laughed with their friends. I had always been a top-of-class student in grammar school, but I sensed this whole high school thing was going to be a long, uphill climb.

Nothing felt familiar or easy during that first year at Neptune High. That much change, and that quickly, wasn't easy. I was proud and happy to be enrolled in the college-preparatory program. On the other hand, very few of my closest friends were in any of my classes. When we arrived at school, we went our separate ways, and it felt uncomfortable not having them around. Subtle differences and tensions began to form as we each began feeling our way into this new situation.

"How were your classes today?" I would sometimes ask them, to get a feel for how things were going in the non-college-preparatory classes, whatever those were.

"Alright," they'd respond, their eyes looking off into the distance. "Nothing to get excited about. But damn, I'll tell you what I can't wait for—football season. Then we'll have some real fun."

As an African American and an athlete, most people assumed I was in a non-academic program, studying some trade like woodworking or carpentry. In the locker room, other players asked me what I was taking and were genuinely surprised to hear my course load included algebra, biology, and English composition. For me, it wasn't really a surprise that they would make such an assumption. Self-doubt and feelings of insecurity about what I was capable of seemed to come with the territory. My college-prep courses were mostly filled with smart students from other white parts of the township, and the fact that they were headed to a good college and a prosperous life felt like a given.

But it wasn't just about the difference of our skin color or what neighborhood we came from. I knew very little about the world they came from, and they knew little about mine. The apparent gap between our cultures felt large but not necessarily conflicting. "Hey, Larry, take it easy and have a good evening." "Yeah, man, you do the same" was often what we said to each other at the end of the school day.

Yet I found myself feeling socially isolated. Maybe it was the distance between our different parts of town. In truth, it felt more substantial than that. Like an invisible barrier existed.

The academic side of the equation was challenging, but I felt up to the task. Even optimistic. But this social situation was very challenging. I wondered if this wasn't a big part of what it meant to be "in the minority," with so few who understood me, and despite my interests or abilities, feeling like I was somehow arriving on the scene with a distinct, yet unnamed, disadvantage.

I reflected on what Mom and Dad had taught us. "It's not the color of a person's skin that's important. Don't judge people based on their circumstances. It's the kind of person they are that's important. Look for the good in others."

Do our parents' teachings and our upbringing really make that much of a difference no matter what side of the track you're from? I wondered. And more to the point, is it even *possible* for me to actually live with that kind of attitude? And how, exactly, am I going to find the strength and self-confidence to live in that way?

One obvious place to start making new friends in high school was on the basketball team. But tryouts for the freshman basketball team were like a stage for the athletic ego. Over a hundred players showed up, and everyone was keen to showcase their talents and claim their place on the team. From the first whistle, guys jockeyed to establish their reputation as a star ball player, though some brought their swagger from grammar school competitions. Fortunately, my grammar school was dominant, so I hoped that helped. Everyone tried to play well, but sounding confident was important too. "I'm better than you, man. Can't you see? You can't stop me."

Basketball is supposedly a team sport. But during tryouts, each player naturally wanted to stand out to make the team, and this became a very confusing situation for me. First of all, talking was not my thing. Secondly, I figured passing the ball to enable an open teammate to score a basket for the team was pretty much what the game was about. However, it soon became clear, in this situation, when another player was open for an easy shot, guys would often take the shot themselves.

"Sorry, man, I didn't see you," they'd shout over their shoulder, as they ran happily back down the court. It became a kind of no-teamwork team sport.

The coaches tended to reinforce this self-centered approach to the game.

"Take the shot, Holmes," was often heard in a loud shout from the bench. Meanwhile, I was thinking, "Yeah, but that guy has a better shot."

Decision. I passed the ball. Wrong decision.

"What are you doing, Holmes? Take the damn shot!"

What to do? More freshman doubt and uncertainty to deal with. Still, I made the team. Mission accomplished. More opportunities to someday become like Elgin Baylor.

Playing high school basketball gave me exposure to a much wider group of players. Meeting guys from different backgrounds, cultures, and ethnic groups was an eye-opening experience for me. My world was expanding, and in a good way. It felt good to be a part of an activity that included so many different kinds of people.

We also started playing ball with older guys at good outdoor courts around town.

"Hey, Larry," I heard one of my friends say after a game. "You should come play some ball with us this summer at the outdoor courts in Ocean Township. There are some awesome players and great pickup games going down there. You'd love it."

Playing with these established players, including some already in college, the pressure was intense. It was a pickup game situation, so you had to be picked by the guy who had called, "I got next." He was allowed to pick the four other guys for his team. The rule was the winning team stayed on, and the losers sat down. Most evenings there were twenty or thirty guys wanting and waiting to play. Losers hoped they would get a second chance to play, but time didn't always allow for that to happen. "You lose, you cruise," was the saying. And if you do lose, the winners were provided the opportunity to look at you bemused and say, "Sit down... chump." You had to prove yourself, and quickly, before you were allowed to play with players at this level. They were the stars from local and state-wide high school teams and some of the nearby colleges, and there was constant commentary from the peanut gallery on the sidelines.

"Hey, isn't that Henry Moore from Neptune High?"

"Yeah, man, he's at Monmouth University now."

"That dude's quick, and it looks like the ball's just part of his hand."

"Yeah, and that's Ron Kornegay. He plays with Henry at Monmouth."

"He's just five-seven, but he's supposed to be too skilled and deceptive to guard."

"Oh damn. Look over there. That's Bob Verga from St. Rose High School. He's the highest scorer in the whole state. No one can stop him from scoring. Your efforts just wind up looking pathetic."

On and on it went. It was great just watching these guys play. But the real challenge was to become a good enough player to be allowed on the court with them.

The physical part of the game was invigorating and exciting, and on the court, I felt more comfortable in my skin than anywhere else. But if I made a mistake, the relentless criticism and one-upmanship could spark an unwelcome bout of self-doubt. I could see it in the eyes and physical reactions of other players. I could also feel it in the tightness of my own body.

And the self-defeating thoughts running uncontrolled through my mind convinced me the mental side of the game was my biggest challenge. Thoughts like: Man, how could I miss such an easy shot? And what's with letting that guy get around me like that? That's not good enough.

These personal doubts were happily amplified by the other players.

In fact, the older guys teased and taunted new guys like me endlessly.

"Hey, why didn't you get that rebound? You're hopeless. You let your man score. Pass the ball, rookie. You can't shoot. Why are you out here?"

And the unwritten rule: we could never question or react to anything they said.

But we also sensed if we kept coming back, put up with the harassment, and continued to develop our skills and—to be fair—our attitude, we might slowly be accepted, and perhaps even acknowledged as an okay player.

"The kid's alright. He can play a little," was what we longed to hear. Translated, this meant something like, "He's a pretty good ball player. I'd pick him for my team."

I knew I wanted to be a part of this "club" of higher-level players. And to do that meant working my butt off and being able to stand up to constant criticism, even from the spectators.

Within this furnace, our love of the game was severely tested.

Is this how acceptance works? I wondered. So slow and begrudging? I played so hard on those outdoor courts, I ran holes in the soles of my sneakers every few weeks. Mom would notice and ask,

"What do you do with these sneakers, son? How can you get through them so often? You need a new pair or you'll be running on bare feet."

Sports were big in school too. If you played sports, people in Neptune knew who you were. There were advantages and disadvantages to that reality. Mostly you were admired and respected. But you were being watched and likely judged as well. Both positively and maybe negatively.

We had a strong basketball tradition at Neptune High. The gym would regularly pack out with fifteen hundred to two thousand people at home games. For games against our local rival, Asbury Park, the games were moved to the famous Convention Hall on the boardwalk to accommodate crowds of up to five thousand spectators. It was always standing room only, and the intensity of this rivalry always held the threat of fights and violence.

During the sixties, Neptune High School produced a steady stream of top teams and basketball players, year in and year out. It was exciting to be a part of some of those championship teams, although never as a star player. Good skills, the love of the game, and a secret but passionate dream of going to college on a basketball scholarship kept my commitment and motivation high.

The drive to be recognized as an exceptional player, like my heroes, made poor performances even more disappointing. Getting stuck in such emotions had a negative impact on my performance and my mental state. I made the junior varsity team my sophomore year and was easily on track to make the varsity team the next year. But the competition within the team was getting more intense too. We were hearing about some incredibly talented and advanced players coming in. They were tall, strong, fast, and on the outside, at least, fearless. As a basketball player at Neptune High School in the 1960s, to make the team, competing against players of this talent level, you had to be good, very good. I was good, especially on defense, which was my special talent. But there were times when my offense was not as consistent, and I lacked the confidence to score against highly-talented teams.

At the end of my sophomore season, my junior varsity coach approached me.

"Hey, Larry, I'd like to talk with you for a minute," he said, in a quiet and concerned tone. "The varsity coach is thinking of cutting you from the team next year. He feels you're too slow. I just wanted to give you the heads up."

What? Cut me? Could that be true?

I felt my legs going weak. My mind struggled to imagine not being on the team. Basketball was my love and inspiration. The thing I did to get me through the tough times in life.

At that moment, I felt a huge void inside myself.

Silently ringing in my ear, I heard the sideline critics' voices. "You're no good. You don't have any game. You're just a chump."

Then my inner voice. "Too slow? Then why does everyone keep telling me my speed and quickness to the ball are my special talents? Tell me that, huh?"

Egos are frail in high school. To hear that news as a fifteen-year-old, the youngest in my class, and totally passionate about basketball, it felt pretty much like a death stroke.

For a few days, I didn't know what to do.

But just as it seemed the night couldn't get any darker, something rather remarkable happened. The same junior varsity coach who had given me the bad news came up with a suggestion.

"You know, Larry," he said, "our varsity team is undefeated and headed to the state tournament. They're gonna need some good players to play the role of the opposition in their training sessions leading up to the games. Would you like to be on that practice squad?'"

"Yes. Yes, please!" I responded in a heartbeat.

"Great," he said with a grin. "I'll suggest that to the varsity coach."

I was so surprised that he asked me. I was jumping up and down inside. In the blink of an eye, everything had turned around.

For the next three weeks, I competed with our incredibly talented varsity team, who hadn't even come close to losing through twenty-five games. I listened to the instructions and guidance of the coaches, tried to apply it, and slowly became more capable of competing at a higher level. I was back to playing against players who were better than me.

In the middle of all my high school sports challenges, another ray of light appeared—Henry Moore. Henry was a recent graduate of Neptune High, and an incredibly talented, smart, and electric basketball player. He had a spark that made his game exciting to watch. He openly acknowledged he had some physical shortcomings, but he was never going to be limited by them. He was so skillful and smart that if a team tried a full-court press, either man-to-man or zone, the coach would simply say, "Give the ball to Henry and get out of the way." Press broken.

Henry understood the gauntlet-like dynamics that make it difficult to succeed as a ball player in a local high school. To my surprise, he approached me after practice one day and said, "Hey, you know you have a good game of basketball. I really admire your game. You play with intelligence."

I couldn't believe someone as amazing as Henry was even talking to me, let alone telling me I was good.

"But," he continued, "you lack confidence. You've got to believe in yourself as a player. There's always gonna be guys at you, saying hyper-critical things when you miss a shot or play a bad game. Don't limit yourself based on their criticism. Don't listen to them if they don't have anything to give you that can help you."

Yeah, I thought to myself, I've been trapped by what other people think of me.

"Who you listen to is important," Henry said. "Everyone has an opinion. What matters is who comes to you with light. People who offer you love and support and wisdom. Those are the people to listen to."

Henry Moore was one of those people. I didn't know anything about philosophy or psychology when I was fifteen. I just wanted to play basketball. But wanting is not always enough. The real question is, how do you achieve what you want?

I took what Henry said to heart and worked hard on my skills and started to observe my thinking too. This was one of the first big wake-up calls in my basketball game, and in my life.

The next year, I didn't get cut from the team. In fact, I made the starting five!

Another unexpected light appeared about that time in my life. Stan wasn't from my school. In fact, he was from one of our main cross-town rivals, Asbury Park High. But we both played in the local VFW marching band, so we started hanging out together based on our musical connection. We would listen to and talk about music of all kinds. Slowly we drifted into discussing the social and party scene, news, politics, civil rights, counterculture, and a bunch of topics I knew very little about.

Stan didn't play a sport, but he could totally relate to someone performing at the top of their game. "Wow!" I said one day. "Kareem is incredibly talented and skillful for a player his size. He's radically changing the role of seven-foot players."

"Now that's interesting," Stan responded with genuine interest and a barrage of penetrating questions. "So, what's so unique about his skill, and why haven't other big men done what he's doing? Where's he from? What's his family background?" Before I could answer, he was off on another track. "What are the major influences in his life, like his parents? Who are the other big men, especially black ones, that he's competing against? What do they think of Kareem's success? How do they assess his early accomplishments?"

And just like that, Stan's questions sparked a rich and lively two-hour conversation on the influences—family history, education, personality, mindset, and even politics—that play a role in whether or not you become a great sportsman.

Stan was a voracious reader, and as our friendship grew, he took to coming by my house on Sunday mornings with *The New York Times*. The first time he showed up with it, I was shocked to see a newspaper of that bulk. The thing was so huge I figured it must take a week to read it. He plonked it down on the floor in my room in the basement of our house, and all I could say was, "Whoa! Do you actually read all that?"

He smiled, shrugged bashfully, and said, "It's one of my bad habits."

It soon became a favorite part of our week, reading articles to one another, and talking for hours on end about whatever subjects flowed from them.

After reading a long article about Martin Luther King Jr., he started in.

"So, Larry, how do you think Martin Luther King's approach compares with other civil rights leaders of our time?"

And off we went, exploring his question together, as he casually provided observations about the views of Stokely Carmichael, Malcolm X, Huey Newton, and the Black Panthers. Then we'd compare them with the more traditional strategies of groups like the NAACP and the Black Caucus.

When we got into these long conversations, Stan's amazing observations and comments prompted me to reflect more deeply. Was it possible to really grasp and understand so many different and apparently conflicting perspectives of life with such clear-headed thinking and begin to see potential ways of making things better?

It was a new and heady experience, and thanks to Stan's influence, it soon became undeniably clear that there was way more to America and the world than our little community of Neptune or even the excitement of New York City, for that matter. Stan showed me just how many people, places, and cultures there are in the world with something different, unique, and interesting to offer us, and this became the spark that inspired me to open my eyes and look at all three-hundred-sixty degrees of the world around me.

"I'm really fascinated with Brazil," he said one day, after reading an article in the *Times* travel section. "Its culture is so different from ours. I want to experience it."

The following week he shared his detailed plans for a year-long trip to Brazil. This see-and-then-do attitude was Stan at his best. His openness and expansive view of life began to sink into my way of looking at things.

Tensions were steadily building between whites and blacks across the country during my high school years in the early 1960s. One incident in particular really got my attention. Four young black college students at North Carolina A&T, a historically black college in North Carolina, sat down at a Woolworth's "Whites Only" lunch counter and ordered coffee. They were told to leave. They were refused service. They continued to sit there. That was the start of the Greensboro sit-ins. I was really affected by this event. It felt so wrong that such separation existed in our country. The awkward part was that we couldn't—or at least didn't feel—we could talk about all this in our classes at school. Everyone knew it was happening. But we all just sat there with our mouths shut, confused and unsure if we should raise the subject. How could we, in mixed company?

"So, did you guys hear about how those black students were refused service at the Woolworths? What do you think about that?"

I could only imagine the total silence that would likely follow such a question. Of course, as soon as us black students were by ourselves, it was the first and loudest topic of conversation.

At home, things were different. At home, there was always talk. Loud talk. As the first home in our neighborhood to have a TV, folks often came around to our place to watch the news. Mid-sentence, the unsuspecting newscaster would be unceremoniously upstaged by someone from the growing party standing around our television.

"Did you hear about that black guy? What's his name?" someone asked.

"James Meredith. Yeah. That's it," another added.

"They ain't never gonna let that black man into that white college. No way."

In this way, a running commentary began on an unpredictable range of current events and issues. It was 1962, during my sophomore year of high school, and the Supreme Court had just ordered the University of Mississippi to admit their first black student, James Meredith. Governor Ross Barnett refused to allow Meredith entry. That afternoon when I got home, the news had broken.

"Did you hear that? The president stepped in."

"President Kennedy ordered US marshals to escort James Meredith."

"He got his own escort into the University of Mississippi?"

There was stunned silence around the TV room as it all sank in. Just to make sure it was true, we and certainly most other black folks were glued to the TV news that night. I was looking to enter college in two years' time. This was, in fact, becoming personal.

"Well, I never," one of my aunts said. "I never thought it would happen. Never thought I would live to see the day."

In contrast, not long afterwards, Medgar Evers, the field marshal for the National Association for Advancement of Colored People (NAACP), was assassinated.

"You see. I told you so."

"They may let one man into their white college, but look at this."

"That's just what they do to black people."

"This has been going on forever."

"People up North never knew."

"The world over, they never knew. It wasn't on TV."

"Maybe white folks think it's time to let black people go to these white colleges?"

"Nah, you really think they're gonna let him in? Just like that?"

"Well, they don't *need* to do anything for him, since he's black. They don't *want* to do anything for him, and they ain't *never gonna do* anything for him."

"They ain't gonna let him in. You just wait and see." And on it went.

My older brother, Al Junior, would start in with the questions, in that quiet intense way of his. "Why do you think they would let Meredith into that college?"

"Well, it's the right thing to do and it's about time."

And no matter the answer, Junior would pose another, more challenging question: "Do you think those white parents really want a black man in that all-white college with their young sons and daughters? Do you think they would be comfortable with that situation?"

These kinds of question-and-answer sessions with Al Junior could go on for hours. As a youngster, it really made me think and question my own assumptions about what was really going on in people's minds and hearts. Over the years, he became infamous for his constant questioning to get to the root of an issue. "Why are you doing that? Is that your best option? Who are you going with? When are you coming back?" We were quizzed to the nth degree, and he often drove us crazy. But we also laughed about it. At least when we weren't the one being interrogated.

Television was good for black people. Racial issues and violence were beamed into our homes on the nightly news for the first time. TV showed marchers being hosed down by firemen and police using vicious dogs to attack them. Television helped expose the inequities in American society.

All over the country and the world, people began asking questions.

"Is this us attacking our own peaceful demonstrators? Is this the kind of country and people we are?"

Abroad, people were asking, "What is it really like in America? How could they allow such brutal actions against their own people?"

The Civil Rights Movement was sparked by a multitude of violent, cruel, and vicious incidents that were made public, mainly through television. In "living color," it reflected a moral crisis for the US. Many wondered if we as a nation would make good on the lofty rhetoric of our origins, steeped in high moral platitudes about the land of the free and home of the brave. As black people, that wasn't our day-to-day experience. It would take real courage to face this challenge, for everybody.

As I thought about the history being made every day in our country, it seemed to be more an issue of human rights than just civil rights. Whatever you called it, this was the climate we grew up with in the '50s and '60s. These happenings and the endless conversations they spawned were the backdrop to our teenage years.

I love this country; it's my home, I thought. But at the same time, how can people be treated like this? There has got to be a way to stop this but I had no idea how. There were so many questions spinning around in all of our heads. What is right and fair? Do all white people hate all black people? Should we hate anyone who hates us? Should we be angry, sad, or just silent?

The answers didn't come easily, if at all.

Into this environment stepped a man who was to become a real hero in my eyes. His name was Martin Luther King Jr. He emanated such rare intelligence and had an ability to artfully articulate his points of view. He was brave beyond question. But more than anything, he believed in humanity and its capacity to right the wrongs that were taking place. He could talk about the issues in a way that brought clarity and allowed many to reframe their perspective on race issues in America. His teaching was simple: you can't fight hate with hate, or darkness with darkness. If you do, you'll simply be creating more of what you want to change…multiplied exponentially. You fight darkness with light, hate with love. If you become like your oppressor, where will that lead? You will simply become the oppressor, in another form.

Martin Luther King Jr. was somehow able to be against the injustices of our society without being against the people perpetrating them. That struck me as being very true and very powerful. In my head, I would compose inspiring talks to deliver like King,   in the same way that all kids like to imitate their heroes.

In my junior year of high school, Martin Luther King Jr. was arrested and sent to jail in Birmingham, Alabama, for protesting the treatment of black people. In those days, if you mentioned Birmingham to most black people, they would say, "Birmingham, Alabama? Oh no, I'm not going there," even though there was a significant black population in Birmingham. Hence the reason for having the demonstrations there.

It was terrifying to watch the news footage. Would I have the courage to participate in such a demonstration? I didn't think so, but I wished I could be that brave. Maybe one day.

Birmingham, Alabama, was one of those places that brought up terrible images, especially for us in the North. Martin Luther King Jr. penned his famous "Letter from Birmingham Jail" there, and in it, he wrote,

> Non-violent direct action seeks to create such a crisis and foster such a tension that a community, which has constantly refused to negotiate, is forced to confront the issue.

I had never encountered such a unique way of thinking and speaking. To me, it suggested that there was a deep connection between races, beyond color. His words felt like they contained new possibilities and hope that resonated deeply within me.

In August of 1963, backing up his Birmingham letter, King delivered his even more famous and soaring "I Have a Dream" speech to 250,000 people in Washington, DC. Glued to the television, we watched and marveled at his profound words of wisdom.

> When we allow freedom to ring, when we let it ring from every village and every hamlet, from every state and every city, we will be able to speed up that day when all of God's children, black men and white men, Jews and Gentiles, Protestants and Catholics, will be able to join hands and sing in the words of the old Negro spiritual: "Free at last. Free at last. Thank God Almighty, we are free at last!"

The inclusiveness of his language offered a compelling challenge and mandate to include and heal all of us in the great American dream. Yet another light in the darkness.

In September that year, an African American Baptist Church in Birmingham was bombed, and four young girls were killed. Outside, I was observing a roller coaster of events. Inside, I felt a range of confusing feelings. I was angry and fearful that such things were still happening in the home of freedom and opportunity. I wondered how such violence could be happening in our country, and what I could I do to help change things. But who am I, anyway?

In November of that year, President John F. Kennedy was assassinated. It felt like it was going from bad to worse.

What were the white kids in my high school classes thinking about all this? It was not like they came up to me and said, "Hey Larry, did you see the news last night? Wasn't that horrible what those folks did to those black kids?" Mostly, my classmates were nice, but I didn't know where they really stood on these issues. I certainly didn't know what was being said by their folks at home. I learned or chose to keep quiet. And I didn't know if that was a good thing or not.

Toward the end of my junior year, our history teacher gave us an assignment, allowing us to choose a history topic and give our own point of view. In the process of doing research, I found a real sense of passion about my subject. It was a good essay and I turned it in with pride in what I had written. When our teacher returned the essays, I didn't get mine.

After class, he looked at me with a stern face and said, "Larry, you need to stay behind after class ends, I need to speak with you." He was a tall, imposing, and no-nonsense figure, almost as if he stepped out of a distant past, where those in charge were always right. This thought unsettled me, and the look on his face caused my stomach to churn. So many thoughts went through my mind. None of them were comforting. Why does he want me to stay behind? Why didn't he return my report? Could it be that bad?

"Who wrote this?" he asked. And before I could mumble a response, he added, "Obviously, not you. You're not capable of this quality of work."

This was a shocking statement of condemnation, and it caught me completely off guard. How did he know what I was capable of?

"Excuse me, sir. What?" I offered meekly.

Internally, I was steaming and thinking: What the hell? After all the work I put into this paper, and this is your response? Really? He didn't ask what inspired me to put so much work into my report. He was simply and calmly certain it was not my work, because of its quality. I wondered why. My work had been pretty good. Not the best, but good.

It felt like a cruel and unfair accusation. His words had a sting to them and rang in my head, "You're not capable of doing this quality of work. What do you have to say for yourself?"

"I wrote this, sir."

What else could I say? There was so much confusion inside me. I did the research and wrote the paper on my own. Why would my teacher doubt me?

"When you're ready to tell me the truth," he said, "come see me."

I knew my teacher was wrong. But for some reason, he was convinced he was right. Our interactions made me feel small, embarrassed, and powerless to do anything about it, and this became a catalyzing experience for me. I felt angry and unseen but with no obvious way to express these emotions. Feelings of self-doubt mixed with my anger and created confusion. Did he think I was not smart enough for some reason? Was I somehow inferior to the other students? At the same time, I thought to myself: You don't know me.

What right do you have to judge me? It felt like a healthy reaction.

I felt a fire being lit within and a deep question posed—who am I, really? What's the truth about me? The cruel poison of prejudice had made itself known in a very personal way for me—for perhaps the first time.

During that same semester, my youthful English teacher took a very different approach. English had been my second-least favorite subject after history. To me it had always been about grammar, which felt like a lot of complicated and unnecessary rules about how to speak. Speaking wasn't really that complicated. I'd been doing it my whole life pretty well without knowing or understanding all the rules of grammar.

But at the beginning of this school year, in walked a fresh-faced young man with a smile on his face and a perk in his step. He wanted to talk about how great—and often old—literary works could relate to our lives today. That caught my interest.

Out of the blue, after class one day, he casually approached and said,

"Hey, Larry, there's a great movie playing called *West Side Story*. Have you seen it? You might like it." It was so surprising for him to say that.

"I haven't heard anything about it," I responded.

"It's a great story, and it's a musical," he added

"Oh," a tinge of doubt rose up inside, "a musical? Really?"

I remembered watching musical movies on TV. Not exactly my favorites.

"Give it a try," he suggested. "I think you might really like it."

So I did. To my great surprise, the music was brilliant. I felt like getting out of my seat to join their dances. And the story felt real and meaningful to me because it reflected the challenges and struggles I saw playing out in my life and the lives of people all around me in my hometown. It captured the sense of roughness and the danger of hanging out on the streets, especially when local tough guys were roaming around. Like Russian roulette—you didn't know when the next bullet would take away a friend or a family member.

During my senior year, there was an incident that reflected these gang-like racial and neighborhood tensions that were often just below the surface. Neptune High regularly had very good basketball teams, with highly talented and athletic players. There were times when, against less talented teams, we would win games by as many as fifty points. That's a lot when you're only playing four, eight-minute quarters. We enjoyed winning big, but no high school kid likes to be embarrassed in front of their friends and family by losing by forty or fifty points.

On one occasion, we were playing a high school in our conference called Freehold. We would tease that they were just a country school out in the sticks. At the time, this was true. We had just finished a game at their school and had won handily. I was a bit slower coming out of the locker room after showering and getting dressed, only to find chaos as I walked out of the building. Our players were running about and shouting,

"Quick, get on the bus, we gotta get out of here. They're coming after us!"

"What's happening?"

"We'll tell you on the bus. Get going, man!"

I ran to the bus and hopped on. All the guys were so excited and trying to talk at the same time. Most of them stood up and leaned over the back of seats, forming a huddle. The rest were shouting from their seats, giving their version of the story.

"Man, you should have seen it. Bob walked out and they just jumped him."

Bob Davis was our star player on the basketball team. He was a star player on the football team and the baseball team too. He eventually became an NFL quarterback. He was that kind of gifted and talented athlete. Not only was he a gifted athlete, but he was called "the golden boy." He gave off that aura. He was tall, smart, handsome, and athletic. He also had a nice personality and dated the captain of the cheerleading squad. You could say he had the whole package. If there was someone who seemed to represent the gulf between the haves and the have-nots, it was Bob Davis.

"So, Bob comes out of the changing room after the game," one guy says.

"And a bunch of guys from Freehold jumped on him," another adds.

"Yeah, and they just start beating him up, bad," a third chimes in.

"So, our guys saw this, and they ran over to help and chased the Freehold guys down into a room and cornered them."

"'We got 'em now,' someone yelled, and then one of the Freehold guys reached in his pocket and pulled something out."

"He's got a gun!"

"So, all us guys from Neptune High turned and ran hard back to our bus."

Adrenaline was rushing through our veins on the way home, and we were all laughing and shoving each other around as we told and re-told our story to the rest of the team. The incident became the night we won our game, survived a violent attack, and lived to tell the tale. As young men, searching for our manhood, the thrill of such a close encounter with danger felt like a rite of passage.

"Man, that was crazy. We almost got shot. What a rush."

When I came through the back door later that night, Mom noticed a big tear in my pants. I shared our heroic tale, and how my ripped pants were the result of our hasty retreat. For years afterwards, we heard her say, "Whenever they play those Freehold boys, they always get in a fight. It's so dangerous."

It only happened once, but the experience stuck with me, too, and hung around in my mind like a warning of uglier things to come.

By senior year of high school, I was eager to move on with my life. Not because it was so bad, but because it somehow didn't feel complete or fulfilling enough. I sensed there were possibilities for a more expansive experience of life elsewhere, and the time was drawing near to gather my courage and explore what the wider world offered for my future. My two best hopes of connecting with these possibilities seemed to be through college and sports. The offer of an athletic scholarship to attend a good university was my dream—to keep playing in college while studying. It would also allow me to relieve some of the financial pressure on my parents to pay for my education. Fulfilling this goal would be the best of both worlds. The notion was exciting and more than a little nerve racking. But mostly, it was highly motivating to reach for the next level in my game. My ticket into a larger, more expansive world.

FULL CIRCLE

3

THAT DON'T MAKE NO KINDA SENSE!

Instead of running up and down the basketball court, football fields, or baseball diamonds, hundreds of thousands of guys my age were hacking their way through jungles, seeking to engage and eliminate the Vietcong guerrilla fighters. And television brought the war into our nation's living rooms in living color.

In our family, college was stressed as the way out of the cycle of oppression and poverty, which was the plight of so many black people in those days in America. Dad made this point abundantly clear. He was determined that we all get a college education. Mom and Dad never backed away from that position, even though Mom didn't express it with as much fervor.

Whenever a conversation turned to the future for their children, my parents made it clear: "Study hard. Don't be like us. We never even finished grammar school, so life has been hard for us."

On the other hand, to Dad, basketball meant very little, and perhaps more importantly, he thought mixing sports with study was a bad idea and a dangerous distraction. He saw sports as something that kids who weren't very bright or motivated used as a way of avoiding what was *truly* important in life. He saw this as being especially the case with black kids. For him it was like chasing a dream that was very unlikely to come to fruition. This made a lot of sense because it was long before the days of big multi-million-dollar professional contracts.

"Forget about basketball and focus on your study," Dad preached on a regular basis when I was a teen. There was truth in what he was saying, I knew. But it certainly wasn't what I wanted to hear at the time.

For the first six games of my senior season, I was playing really well. I wasn't one of the stars, but in my role as the primary defensive guard against the oppositions' top scoring guard, I was in peak form. And I was scoring in double figures too. Plus, we were undefeated. This was fun. My dream come true.

But the dream didn't last long. That year, we were playing in a Christmas holiday tournament at the fancy Asbury Park Convention Hall on the boardwalk. It was the place where all the big games were played, primarily because you could typically squeeze almost five thousand screaming students and spectators into it—with standing room only.

We were undefeated and so was our opponent, Saint Rose, a nearby Catholic high school. Normally, playing against a Catholic high school would be easy for us. However, in this case, the added drama and challenge was the fact their team was good, especially because one of their players was the highest scoring player in the entire state of New Jersey. He was averaging close to 40 points a game.

As I was the defensive stopper on our team, I was given the task of trying to stop or at least slow him down. Our coach's strategy was for me to use my quickness to keep him from getting the ball, and if he did get it, play him tight, and maybe get some help from my teammates. In the incredibly fast-paced first half, I felt a step too slow and allowed him to score 20 points. Not good. At that pace, he was on track to score his normal 40 points, or more. After some halftime strategy adjustments and a mental reset, my head was more in the game. With an inspired effort, I held him to only two points in the third quarter. Every time their star player got the ball, the Neptune student crowd cried out with deafening screams, "Defense, Defense!" My confidence soared, and he only scored eight more points in the final quarter. Not much by his standards. And an exceptional defensive effort on my part. Unfortunately for our team, and me in particular, those points came at critical times, and we lost the game. Overall, my effort was considered the best defense anyone had played against him. But Neptune High basketball and its longtime coach didn't usually lose such games. This was the beginning of a reshuffle of the lineup by our coach. To our surprise, at Monday's practice, a couple of highly talented freshmen joined our varsity squad. One of them was inserted into the starting lineup in my place. It was an extraordinarily bitter pill for me to swallow.

My dad's response to my not playing as much as I had was swift and uncompromising.

"If you're going to be sitting on the bench and not playing a lot, it's just a waste of your time. First of all, I don't feel like your coach is being fair with you. I've never played basketball, or any sport for that matter, but you look as good as the other players to me. You need to get on with your studies and prepare for college, son."

"But I love playing, Dad," I implored with dismay and a catch in my throat. "I mean, I think I'm good enough to play in college too… maybe even get a scholarship."

"I want to talk to your coach, son," responded Dad, in his typical straight forward fashion. "I want to see what he thinks about your possibilities."

His response caught me completely off guard. For one thing, I couldn't imagine my dad and my coach even being in the same room together, let alone it leading to any kind of productive conversation. It made me nervous just thinking about their potential interactions. Worst case scenario—which actually seemed quite possible—was that Dad would lose his temper and wind up yelling at our coach, and I'd get kicked off the team.

Much to my trepidation, the meeting took place, and to my genuine surprise, Dad was calm but firm. He began by firing a volley of statements in rapid succession at my coach.

"First off, let's get something clear, Coach," he began. "Larry likes playing basketball, but going to college is his top priority. So, if you're not going to play him much, then he's wasting his time sitting on the bench when he could be studying."

He paused to make sure he'd been clearly heard and understood.

"Do you think," he continued, with a little less bravado, "my son is a good player? Good enough to play in college, even though he's not a star on this team?"

"Yes," my coach responded with zero hesitation.

Really? I was dumbfounded and thrilled, all in the same wonderful moment.

"Yes, Mr. Holmes, I do think so," my coach continued earnestly, "if you choose the right college."

"OK," my dad said evenly. "How can you help him do that?"

What's going on here? I wondered. Who is this guy? And what have you done with my father?

"Well," Coach continued, "just let me know the colleges Larry's most interested in attending. I'll contact their coaches and let them know what a talented player he is."

Whoa. I was in shock. Could this really be happening? By the look on his face, Dad was a bit surprised too. I felt something turn in the universe and in our relationship.

"Larry," I heard my coach say, "give me the names of the colleges next week, and I'll write the letters and get this process going."

Seven weeks later, Mom brought the mail in the side door to the kitchen and handed me an official-looking letter from Fairleigh Dickinson University. Damn, I thought, that's a Division I university in upstate New Jersey. What could it be?

"What could it be?" Mom asked aloud. "Are you going to open it dear?"

I did.

"Dear Larry...The Fairleigh Dickinson University Athletics Department is pleased to offer you a basketball scholarship for the coming..."

What! Was this happening? Was my dream coming true?

"They're offering me a basketball scholarship, Mom."

"Oh," Mom said with a sweet smile, "that's nice, dear."

It felt like a new life was beginning—I could get out of my little hometown, play college basketball, get an education, and ease the financial load on my parents. As I stood there looking at the letter, imagining my future, Dad walked in. He listened as I told him the news, nodded his head, and asked, "What are you going to study, son?"

"Oh," I said, realizing I hadn't really gotten that far. "I'll probably just start by studying liberal arts for the first year or two, see what's on offer, and then decide on a major."

Honestly, I had absolutely no idea what I wanted to do with my life. But then, who does at seventeen?

Dad's response was immediate and severe. "That's the dumbest idea I've ever heard in my life, son. That don't make no kinda sense! You should major in something like science. Physics would be a good major. You should major in physics, son."

I was shocked at the force of his response. Here he was trying to push me into something he really didn't know anything about. More importantly, I didn't really want to do that.

"Dad," I reiterated with some trepidation, "waiting to declare your major is a really common thing to do if you're not sure what course of study you want. Lots of people do it."

"Son," he continued, undeterred, "that just doesn't make any sense at all to me. You'd just be wasting your time and a lot of money."

I was intimately familiar with that stern face and unyielding tone of voice but felt compelled to try one more time.

"But Dad, I'll also be playing basketball, and that's gonna take a lot of time and energy too. Besides, I'll have plenty of time to decide on my major even after my first year."

"Well," he said, with his jaw firmly set, "it's nice that you have a scholarship, son, but basketball isn't going to provide a job after you graduate. Physics would really be a good choice. I really think you should major in physics."

He clearly wasn't budging from his position, and I knew a contracted argument with him was only going to leave me feeling more frustrated, angry, and stuck. In retrospect, I should have excused myself and walked away. Instead, I found myself thinking about how much I actually liked my high school physics classes. I especially liked the way it explained how the physical universe works. On the other hand, I wondered if I could hack it at the college level? And also, what do people who study physics actually do for a living? This is not a good idea, my instincts shouted. But I didn't listen. Instead, I heard myself saying, "Okay, Dad, I'll major in physics."

I entered Fairleigh Dickinson University in September of 1964 on a basketball scholarship, with a major in physics. Upon arrival at FDU, I was greeted very warmly by the assistant basketball coach, Ed, a short, bespectacled, middle-aged guy who reminded me more of a professor than a coach.

"Hey, Larry, it's great to have you here," he began with genuine enthusiasm. "We're really looking forward to having a great year. Including you, we've got ten scholarship players on the freshmen team this year! Let me show you around campus and then I can take you over to where you'll be living."

Campus consisted of a circle of a few classroom buildings and a dining hall with the gym above it.

"You probably want to see where you're going to be playing first, right?" Coach Ed offered. I did. It was like finally stepping into the dream I'd imagined for so long.

I felt a chill of excitement as we climbed the stairs and entered the gym—my first look at the hallowed ground of my potential greatness in the sporting universe.

The music stopped, and I woke from my dream with a start, realizing, Oh, this is quite a bit smaller than my high school gym.

Nevertheless, I'd arrived, and I was ready for the new adventure.

"So," Coach Ed continued with unbridled enthusiasm, "let's go take a look at where you'll be living."

"Oh yeah," I asked, "where are the dorms?"

"Well," he answered cheerfully, "there aren't actually any dorms for boys...yet. But," he added quickly, "we've arranged a home for you to live in with a very nice couple."

That caught me by surprise. "I'm going to stay in someone's home?"

"You'll have your own room. Plus, it's just a short walk down the hill from here."

I felt my stomach tighten a bit with the uncertainty of the situation.

"Hop in," Coach Ed said with a grin. "I'll drive you down."

A country mile later, we arrived at a quaint little home at the bottom of the hill.

Oh boy, I thought, an uphill walk to classes and practice every day.

Coach Ed introduced me to the polite elderly couple hosting me. They showed me my compact room, and I moved my things in.

Well, I thought, sitting down to take in my new digs, college life may not be as straightforward as I thought it would be. What about late-night fun in the dorm with my friends? What about hanging out with my teammates after practice? What about doing homework together? Still, I figured, living my dream has got to be worth all the sacrifices. I couldn't wait for practices to start.

In the next few days, I met the other first-year players. We organized unofficial pickup games and started to get to know each other and the skills and experiences we were bringing. They came mostly from the highly competitive New York, New Jersey, Pennsylvania areas. The other two black players, Reggie and Tim, came from the same high school in Plainfield, New Jersey. The other players were a talented mixture of sizes and skills who had been strategically recruited and offered scholarships. They had all been key players on their respective teams, except me. The other guards were great shooters, especially Al, who was deadly. I wasn't sure what I could add to the mix.

We had the pieces to be a good team. But we needed a coach to provide cohesiveness and to build teamwork. There was a real buzz about our new coach, but we had yet to meet him because he had a day job in insurance. His name was Vinnie Ernst, and his reputation preceded him. An all-American player out of Providence College, he was young—just twenty-four years old—and short, for a basketball player. He was only five-eight but solidly built, and straight out of *GQ Magazine*—fair skin, blond hair, and immaculately dressed in Brooks Brothers suits and highly shined brogue shoes. His hair appeared permanently perfect no matter how much sweat poured off his brow. His boundless charisma and youthful energy filled the small gym on FDU's Rutherford, New Jersey, campus. The word went out around campus, and students came to watch our practices, mainly to see him. "Whoa, this dude is so good. Did you see what he just did? And so cool too."

When he was in college, he was known for his incredible speed, quickness, shooting ability, and ball-handling skills. He'd actually made the final cut with the legendary Boston Celtics, and some of the guys were gushing, "He's awesome, man. I saw him play on TV, and he was just a blur."

Our first day of practice rolled around in mid-November. With boyish looks, Coach Ernst burst into the gym, immaculately dressed in a three-piece suit, issuing full-throated orders, egging us on, and smiling all the while. To him, it was all just a big game...which, of course, it was. That caught my attention more than anything.

He talked like he was one of us. "Okay, guys, let me see what you can do. Show me something," which was quite intimidating since he was so much better than any of us. We were totally engaged before he'd done anything, and then he started demonstrating the moves he wanted us to practice— still in his street clothes and dress shoes—and his speed and skill were a thing of beauty. We just looked at each other and silently mouthed, "Damn. You gotta like his style!" We knew we were in for a wild ride, but with his playful personality, we also sensed it was going to be a lot of fun.

I took some pride in being known as a quick player. But against Coach Ernst, I felt like I was moving in slow motion. He had a way of saying things that caught your attention in a direct, easy-to-understand, and difficult-to-ignore way.

If one of us was shooting impulsively and missing, he'd offer,

"That's right. That's right. When in doubt, just shoot the ball. That works, doesn't it? Guys, you have to use your brains to be really good at this game. Run that play again. The right way this time!"

His sarcasm wasn't lost on us. We all cracked up, and so did he. He could yell, but he never really seemed angry, just hopeful that we would learn something.

He made us run so hard and for so long.

"Run. Get those arms up. Hey, there's no car coming to give you a ride. Lift those legs. Ignore the fatigue and pain. Keep going!"

He always had an encouraging smile on his face, like he knew something that we didn't. Which he did. At the end of practice, we dropped to the floor in total exhaustion, too tired to even get a drink of water. During most of pre-season training, I was so sore and so tired, I was sure I'd lost all ability to play the game and would likely never regain it. But just before the season began, the soreness seemed to miraculously go away, and in its place, I discovered my new, stronger, and faster body.

He may have been a young, first-time coach, but none of us had any doubt about how good he was, and how much better we were becoming as players, and as a team, thanks to him.

In addition to giving us new bodies, he taught us how to understand and play the game at a whole new mental and strategic level.

"If the defense tries to pressure you, your response shouldn't be to hesitate or back off. Always attack pressure. That will surprise them. They won't be expecting it, and that's the weakness of their strategy. Playing so close to you, they are vulnerable to a quick or aggressive move. But you have to be bold and fearless. And you have to develop your skills. It takes a strong body and a strong mind."

"Can you teach me, Coach?" became my mantra.

"Absolutely," was always his quick response. "Let's start with one of my favorite drills. Take the ball the full length of the court. We'll put three guards on you, and your job, Larry, is to get by them and score. Piece of cake," he said with a devilish grin on his face.

Then he demonstrated exactly what he had just said. He took the ball full court, weaving in and out of players with such foot speed and dribbling skill it looked like my teammates' feet were nailed to the floor. But I immediately got the connection between what he was saying and what he did. Speed, skill, and the most important element of all: total confidence. That year, I dedicated myself to working on all three. It changed my experience of playing basketball in the most visible and fun way.

I was one of the smaller players and was quietly concerned the taller college players would be able to take advantage of me. Reading my mind, Coach Ernst offered,

"Larry, you have to develop exceptional dribbling skills and use your foot speed and quickness as an advantage to counter their size. Lots of big guys think size is an advantage, so they tend to underestimate what smaller guys like us can do. Look what I've been able to achieve, and I'm shorter than you."

"Thanks, Coach," I said, feeling encouraged.

"You're a very good defensive player, Larry. That's your strength. But you can't just rely on that one skill. Let me help you develop your other skills too, and then your versatility will become your greatest strength."

"Okay, Coach," I said, "but what about my shooting and rebounding? Sometimes it feels like my smaller size is holding me back."

"Rebounding isn't just about being tall, Larry," he responded with a grin. "You're quicker than most big guys and have a surprisingly high vertical leap. I can show you how to use those strengths to give you an advantage. You can raise up and get to the ball before them. The element of surprise will serve you well. The first thing is to change your thinking. Instead of the obstacles, focus on the possibilities."

Coach Ernst saw both my abilities and my potential more clearly than any coach I'd worked with before. Over the coming weeks and months, he showed me the drills to develop the skills I needed. Going one-on-one with him was always challenging and often embarrassing. But everything he did had a clear purpose—to help each of his players excel at our Division I level. And under his guidance, it felt possible.

When the season started, I was more prepared and performed better than ever. He taught me the skills of the game, yes, but there was also a deeper application: the cultivation of a transformational expectation and mindset. It was the same positive approach to apparent problems that Henry had called *looking for the light*, and the proof, as they say, was in the pudding. I became one of the better rebounders on the team and started to see that what I could uniquely contribute to the team was, in fact, my versatility.

Basketball was a huge part of my young life at FDU. And then, of course, there were my classes. As a physics major, my schedule included chemistry, chemistry lab, calculus, English literature, and physics. It was a daunting load, and except for English, I often felt like I didn't really belong in most of my classes. It was a big worry that I carried in stoic silence. As professors introduced what we would be studying, I took lots of notes. But at times, especially in my physics class, it was as if they were speaking a whole new language…which, for me at least, they actually were.

"…and you'll need to memorize these formulas, the periodic table of elements, the basic laws of physics, these symbols and proofs…." I heard somewhere off in the distance.

I'm in over my head, I thought, just as my new friend, Spaulding, turned toward me, and with his usual earnest excitement pronounced,

"Wow, this is so great. I can't wait to learn all this stuff. Isn't it great, Larry?"

"Um, yeah," I said, half-heartedly.

I was, in fact, excited about learning the laws and mysteries of the larger universe in physics and the elemental forms of matter in chemistry. But everything was coming at me so fast, and I was struggling to take it all in.

Spaulding—who was from a family of nine children in nearby Jersey City—commuted from home each day. His enthusiasm and sense of humor were infectious.

"So, Larry," he whispered enthusiastically in the middle of a physics lecture one day, "do you think Einstein's Theory of Relativity means we can find a way to travel at the speed of light? Wouldn't that be amazing?"

"Sure," I said distractedly, and continued ruminating on the extra practice Coach Ernst had called for later that day in preparation for our big game tomorrow. And when exactly, I wondered, am I ever going to find the time to study and do everything these professors are asking us to do? And what about the fun, social side of college life I've heard so much about? Where does that fit in?

Living off campus, most of my social interactions with other students happened in class or the cafeteria. Much like Neptune High, the small number of black students at FDU gravitated toward the "black table." Mostly out of habit, I guess. It's not that I wanted to just be with the handful of black students, which included some international students from Africa. And it wasn't like white students couldn't sit with us. It was just the table where most of the black or African students sat. When I entered the cafeteria, I heard, "Hey. Larry, come sit here with us." From time to time, a white or European classmate would wander over and ask, "Do you mind if I sit here?"

"Sure, have a seat."

But the tone and facial expressions of some of the people around the table created a subtle but undeniable tension. An awkward discomfort. "Now what are we going to talk about?" was the unspoken question hanging in the air. Inwardly I wanted everyone to feel like they belonged, just as I wanted to be accepted. But it mostly just felt uncomfortable for all of us. Like an unseen force field—a black one. Some brave souls approached, felt it, and just moved on. Others stayed and, more often than not, became friends. This equality and integration thing, I realized, is really hard, and it runs deep.

We talked about a lot of things at our table, including classes, home, sports, relationships, and politics. But inevitably, at some point, our conversations would circle back to the questions of racism in America. This is usually when our talk got loudest.

"Stokely's running his mouth again down at Howard," announced someone.

"Oh yeah, man, Black Power!" another said, raising a fist in the air.

"He just puts more people off," another offered.

The debate was on.

"So, is all that mess really helping us? Or is it just hurting our black asses?"

I looked around to see if other students in the cafeteria were noticing our volume and rhetoric. I felt their nervousness like it was my own.

"They've been sticking it to us for a long time. Why don't we stick it back?"

"That Huey—he's from a tough hood in Oakland, right?"

Nods around the table. "Yeah, man, those Black Panthers carry guns. That's pretty radical."

"How 'bout Malcolm X though? He converted to the Nation of Islam, and they're preaching that the only way blacks can get freedom and equality is to create their own state, separate from whites."

"End racism," someone added, "by any means necessary. Including violence."

"Now that's radical," we thought.

I recalled my junior year of high school, when Martin Luther King Jr. was arrested while leading a civil rights protest in Birmingham, Alabama. City officials had used police dogs and high-pressure fire hoses to violently disperse and arrest the non-violent demonstrators, and shocking images of the cruelty they suffered were fresh in everyone's minds, black and white. I felt a deep sense of disappointment in the country I was so proud of and which

was supposed to be "...the land of the free." A place where...
"All men are created equal and endowed by their creator
with certain unalienable rights, including Life, Liberty, and
the pursuit of Happiness." It was so confusing. A hint of
anger started to arise, like when a referee made a bad call, or
when I felt an opposing player was cheating. This was
disrespecting the game. I was realizing the game of life isn't
always a level playing field. Sometimes the game seems
rigged.

Sports, however, were a welcome haven for me and
many of my friends. In that space, I felt a kind of acceptance
and warmth where I could go to find peace amid all the
social and political turmoil happening around me in the
wider world. We were teammates and friends. We're in this
together, right? The prejudices and barriers weren't so in my
face.

And then a young, cocky, and outspoken African
American boxer appeared on the scene and shook my place
of solace to its roots. Cassius Clay returned home from
winning the boxing gold medal in the 1960 Olympics and
was refused service in a "Whites Only" restaurant in his
hometown of Louisville, Kentucky.

"We don't serve negroes here," a staff member informed
him.

"Well," Clay retorted, "I don't eat them neither."

I laughed out loud when I read that. Clay's famously
sharp, funny, and truth-speaking tongue had been
awakened, and I felt a twinge of something stir in me.

"What am I feeling? I don't think I really like this guy," I
thought to myself. Initially, at least, he seemed a bit too
radical and loud mouthed.

Clay was so upset with being treated that way that he
threw his gold medal into the Ohio River. Not long after, he
joined the Nation of Islam and changed his name to

Muhammad Ali, creating a huge controversy in the sporting and public arena.

Heated arguments after basketball practice became the norm.

"He's the best boxer in the world," one of the guys on the team offered.

"Are you crazy? That was a lucky punch," was the response.

"Sonny Liston's the heavyweight champ for sure," another added.

"All of a sudden, Clay's a Muslim, and his new name is Ali? What's that about?"

"He's disrespecting the title."

"He's disrespecting the country."

"All that bragging—'I am the greatest! I am the greatest!' That's not right."

Yeah, I thought, I don't like what's happening to sports. And why brag about yourself?

Being the shy one, I kept my opinions to myself.

Politics, racism, trash talking in the locker room? What was happening to my safe place? I didn't think it was right. And it was certainly not comfortable.

Boxing was probably my least favorite sport, but as I read more about Ali and even watched some of his fights, I was impressed. He was a super-talented, outrageous fighter in the ring. He was smart, lightning quick, and had style too. I liked that. He used all of his athletic gifts and mental talents in the ring. He even talked—teasing and trash talking mostly—during the fight.

He had the courage to challenge the status quo outside of the ring too. He was abrasive, but insightful. Controversial, but always truthful. Egotistical, but with wit and humor...even poetry. And he could most definitely box.

He made me think. As I was wondering where life was going to take me, I heard him say, "I know where I'm going and I know the truth, and I don't have to be what you want me to be. I'm free to be what I want." That really challenged my more easy-going view of life. He's willing to put all he's won at risk for what he believes to be more important—his moral convictions. Who else is willing to do that? Would I be willing to do that if I had to?

After becoming the heavyweight champion of the world, Ali caused another big stir by refusing to enter the military when he was drafted in 1966. He claimed conscientious objector status based on his religious beliefs.

"No Vietcong ever did anything mean to me," he said brashly, "so why should I go to their country and try to kill them?" That sank deep into my consciousness.

His claim was denied, and he was stripped of his heavyweight title and banned from boxing for three years. Many branded him a coward and traitor to his country. But Ali insisted blacks were not being treated as equals at home, and yet they were being asked to fight and possibly die in a war far from home. After a long court battle, his name was cleared, and he came back to reclaim the heavyweight title three more times.

One day I went with some of my FDU frat brothers to a diner just across the Hudson River from the city. As our fraternity's *de facto* "social director," my extra-large fellow teammate and friend, Reggie, was a party animal and had easily convinced us to "postpone our studies and have a little fun." As we were sitting down, our friend Buddy leaned over and said,

"Oh my God. That's Muhammad Ali at that table over there!"

"Right," we all thought. And then we looked, and sure enough, it was him.

"I'm going to get his autograph," Buddy insisted. "Who's got a pen and paper?"

"No, man, don't disturb him. You might get punched in the face."

We laughed, quietly. But the place had somehow become holy ground, and none of us could find a scrap of paper or a pen to save our lives.

"I'm going over," Buddy announced, standing up.

"I don't need a piece of paper. I'm gonna ask him to sign my ten-dollar bill, and someone in his group surely has a pen."

"What?" we all chimed in. But off Buddy went, and we prepared ourselves for the fall out. He soon returned with Ali's signature, and we couldn't believe it.

"He's a really nice guy. I asked if he'd sign my bill, and he just said, 'No problem, man. It's my pleasure. Don't spend that ten bucks soon, it may be worth a bit more later.' He smiled and asked who was with me, and I pointed over at you guys."

Just then, Ali turned around, smiled, and waved at us. No bravado. No grandstanding. We waved back. His unpretentious presence there, just a few feet away, made me feel like the pressing issues were never really that far away. Especially if you lived across the river from New York City.

America was a vast whirlpool of change during my teenage years in the 1960s, and the fact that so many people couldn't achieve and live out their dreams was becoming increasingly apparent to me. At the same time, the jungles of the Vietnam War appeared to have no regard for distinctions of color, political affiliation, or beliefs. It killed and maimed indiscriminately.

Instead of running up and down the basketball court, football fields, or baseball diamonds, hundreds of thousands of guys my age were hacking their way through jungles, seeking to engage and eliminate the Vietcong guerrilla fighters. And television brought the war into our nation's living rooms in living color.

As the number of troops and bombing raids escalated, so did the number of body bags being returned home for burial. And so did the number of friends and classmates my friends and I lost to the conflict. And for what purpose? I wondered. Perhaps Ali was right—"No Vietcong ever hurt me, so why should I go and fight them?"

Young men like myself, attending college and university, were exempted from serving in the military during the Vietnam War—at least, if we were full-time students with twelve or more credit hours per semester. You still had to register for the draft, but you were classified 2S—S for student—and exempt from being drafted on account of your studies.

For my first few years of college, I was registered with my local draft board and received the automatic exemption as a full-time student without seemingly having to do anything. College and sports were the harbors sheltering me from the ever-rising tide of war.

Playing collegiate basketball was a heady and invigorating experience. But it was also incredibly demanding and time consuming. The mental demands of a university physics curriculum combined with the overwhelming gravity of playing Division I basketball stretched me to a kind of breaking point, both physically and mentally. It was just a matter of time, I thought, and someday, I'll just snap right in two.

My dream-come-true was becoming increasingly unattainable. To relieve some of the pressure and get on top of my studies during my junior year, I dropped my course load to a level below that of a full-time student. Just for a semester, I reasoned. I just need to get my feet back under me.

I was surprised to discover I was no longer eligible to play for the FDU basketball team and felt the rug pulled out from under me. The one saving grace was that I could play on my fraternity's intramural basketball team. Division I ball, it was *not*, but at least I was playing on a regular basis.

Losing my spot on the school team was heartbreaking. But I survived and was trying my best to move forward in some kind of positive way.

And that's when the letter arrived.

It began in a very upbeat kind of way, "Dear Larry, your friends and neighbors have chosen you... to serve your country..."

Your friends and neighbors have chosen you. Cool, I thought, maybe I got some kind of good citizenship award? Or a prize?

"...as a soldier in the United States Army."

Wait. What? The *ARMY*? The meaning reverberated deeper and deeper. Is this a conscription letter? Am I being drafted? What about my student exemption?

Then it dawned on me, as a sickening wave of horror and panic clutched my body. Oh God, I thought, I'm a part-time student now. That automatically makes me available for the draft. How could I have missed that? I'm gonna lose everything.

My decision to drop classes automatically activated my reclassification to 1A—Available for Military Service. It happened quickly and impersonally. The slate containing my most cherished hopes and dreams had been instantly wiped clean. In its place was written: "To be determined."

Like a sudden rainstorm, it all came pouring down into a muddy mess of negative thoughts. What will Mom and Dad think after all the hard work they've put into getting me into college? My sister, Pat, has already lost friends in Vietnam, and now she could lose her brother.

I didn't really know much of the history or circumstances of the "conflict" in Vietnam at the time. Being drafted certainly got my attention, though. Initially, most Americans appeared to approve of US involvement in Vietnam. But as the war marched on, the heavy cost in young American lives and money escalated beyond all predictions, and many Americans began to question the necessity or wisdom of the sacrifices. It was no longer just a news story. And now I found myself on the direct road to the battlefield.

Dad offered some advice.

"Why don't you go to officer's training school, son? At least you can be a leader and have some status when you get out."

On that point, there were some chilling facts to offer my dad.

"That," I explained, "would mean a three- or four-year commitment in the army, instead of the two of an enlisted man. I want to get this over and done with as quickly as I can, Dad."

"Well," he responded, "at least you'd come out with some kind of important position and achievement."

In that regard, I thought, he's actually right. So, why am I so uncomfortable with his well-intentioned suggestion?

"Well," I remembered, "for one thing, Dad, the highest mortality rate for soldiers in Vietnam is that of second lieutenants. That's the level I'd graduate with if I decided to get into officer's training school. Then they'd send me straight to Vietnam to lead a platoon into the jungle."

So maybe, I thought to myself, it's not such a good strategy for me to go into a war zone with a target on my back.

"Well, at least you'd be in charge, son," he offered, without addressing the issue of my safety. That hurt, but also something occurred to me. He and I are focusing on different priorities. Dad clearly wants me to use the situation as an opportunity to improve my station in life, which he and Mom have always emphasized in our upbringing. In whatever stage or area of life, they've always encouraged us to be outstanding. Generally, that made sense, but not in this extreme situation where my life might be at risk. My strong impulse was to make a different choice, which meant going against his suggestion. New territory for me. Come what may, I decided to enter the military at the lowest level, as a draftee.

In what was obviously becoming an unpopular and unwinnable war, I felt caught, "between a rock and a hard place." My timing in getting drafted could hardly have been worse. In November of 1969, the largest antiwar demonstration in American history took place in Washington, DC, as 250,000 demonstrators gathered to call for a withdrawal of our troops from Vietnam. "What have I gotten myself into?" I wondered. I just need to survive these next two years. This could easily be a life-or-death decision, and it has to be my choice. Oh God, is this the right thing to do?

I don't know if I showed it, but I felt like I was caught in a trap with no way out, and I was as frightened as I'd ever been.

On January 21, 1969, I was inducted into the United States Army to serve during the Vietnam war. It was the year of peak US troop involvement with over 500,000 soldiers in the country. It had become the longest and most unpopular war in US history at the time. As soldiers, mostly in our late teens and early twenties, it was becoming increasingly clear we were victims of numerous strategies gone horribly wrong. And there appeared to be no way out.

I followed the written instructions provided by the induction center and gathered the few clothes allowed for a recruit, which included only one set of the basics. I got on the bus in Asbury Park and headed an hour south on the New Jersey Turnpike to Fort Dix Army Base in South Jersey. There were about sixty young men on the bus, and there was an odd, almost deathly, quiet. When we spoke, it was in whispers.

"Hey, what's your name?" "Where are you from?" "Did you get drafted or join up?" "I wonder what all this is going to be like."

Faces tended to be pale and ashen. This was totally unlike any group of 18- to 21-year-olds that I'd been on a bus with before. No matter what we thought, whether we wanted to or not, we were going into the army. I finally understood, experientially, a French phrase I had come across in English class: *fait accompli*. As I sat on the bus, the full weight and gravity of the phrase settled in. I was experiencing "a thing already done."

I had been an interested observer of the war before I was drafted. After receiving my draft notice, I began reading up on and following the developments in Southeast Asia more closely. From history class, I vaguely knew that US involvement in Vietnam started somewhere in the 1950s after the French, who had colonized Vietnam and surrounding areas since the late-1800s, withdrew their troops. We were taught the US wanted to contain the spread of communism. The rationale was that if communism wasn't stopped from spreading into Southeast Asia, nation after nation would fall under communist rule like dominos. Thus, the strategy was known as the domino theory. But was this a real threat? I didn't know. My day-to-day issues were not about the threat of communism. My concerns were much closer to home.

I reflected on the turmoil and tensions that in various ways were already affecting me, my family, and my friends. I was becoming more concerned about whether I would experience equal opportunity and respect in my own country, which I genuinely loved. This was true despite its imperfections; it was still my home. I guess this is the deeper meaning of family, tribe, and country. I accepted and loved it despite it not being perfect.

But those feelings and behaviors should be returned, right? Otherwise, the spoken or unspoken bond is broken and needs to be healed.

In the quiet moments on the bus to Fort Dix, I wasn't sure what it all meant, or what I should believe about the whole crazy situation. What I did know was that fighting this kind of war was like going into someone else's "hood," not being able to recognize or know who was in the rival gang, but hoping to win the battle, which is never a good idea.

Getting off the bus in South Jersey with all the other recruits was the precise moment my world changed from an uncomfortable dream into a prolonged nightmare. The drill sergeant started yelling and screaming the moment our feet hit the ground. "Get over here! Stand up straight! Line up!" Each command was shouted with extreme urgency at top volume, flavored with a wide selection of foul words, and punctuated with a single shrill "Trainee!" at the end of each sentence.

"You better get your shit together, Trainee! Or you're gonna find my foot in a very uncomfortable place, Trainee! Do you understand me, Trainee?" He walked briskly toward the door, stopped, turned swiftly around to face us, and made the first order of business abundantly clear.

"And if any of you worthless morons are wondering whether you might have to serve in Vietnam," he growled with a menacing grin, "the answer is, HELL, YES!" And those words changed everything. This was no game.

4

WE WILL TAKE CARE OF OUR OWN

As I felt my life disintegrating around me, I made a pledge: If I get out of this mess alive—and that's clearly not a given—I want my life to be my own. For better or worse, I decide. No more falling asleep at the wheel.

Every recruit was required to do eight weeks of basic training to learn the basic skills of warfare. But no matter how well we performed, the drill sergeants always found ways to make us wrong or not good enough. They pushed us to our limit. And then they pushed some more. "Drop and give me fifty push-ups" was the standard response to even the most minor of infractions. If anyone hesitated or was tempted to argue their case, the punishment was doubled. "Give me a hundred push-ups, Trainee. NOW!"

The physical challenge was a familiar experience from my years of basketball training. But the psychological demand for total submission was far beyond getting fit for a simple game of basketball. Basic training was unyielding in its intention to break every shred of independent spirit or thinking we harbored. The guiding mode of operation of our military training was the all-important chain of command. Breaking, or even questioning, that chain incurred swift and severe punishments. Do whatever you are told…immediately, because, we were told incessantly, in combat situations, not following an order could result in chaos and potential loss of life.

In basketball, some of our coaches seemed bent on breaking our wills so we'd follow instructions in the heat of the game. "Hey, Holmes. Do what I tell you to do, understand? Sit on the bench next to me and see how it should be done." But in high school and college sports, the stakes were considerably lower, and our responses were in keeping with the situation, "Yeah, Coach, sorry." We were embarrassed, but we recovered. We lived to tell the story.

Training for war was a different universe, and mistakes, we quickly learned, can cause great harm to yourself and others. If we slouched, it was "Stand up, Trainee. Is there something wrong with you?" If we looked an officer in the eye, he hovered millimeters from our faces screaming and spitting, "What are you looking at, Trainee? Don't you ever look at me with that face! Drop and give me fifty push-ups….now, Trainee!"

Make no mistake, these drill sergeants were good at what they did. They made it difficult *not* to get overwhelmed by it all. "Surrender to my will" was clearly their primary goal for us. Their demeanor and physical appearance, including their Smokey-the-Bear hats, all added to an aura of total authority over us. Even their questions had the tone of a direct order. There were no explanations. "Just do it. You know nothing. You're lower than whale shit on the bottom of the ocean!"

A series of small but significant rituals took place during our induction into the army. We were ordered to the post barbershop for a haircut. As I reached the front of the line and sat down in the chair, the barber smiled politely and asked,

"How would you like it cut today, son?" I paused and looked around. Everyone was being asked this same question. Regardless of their answer, however, everyone got the same treatment—an astonishingly quick buzz cut, followed by a loud, "Next!" and a belly laugh.

"The standard cut, please," I mumbled, and felt any sense of dignity slip into the ether.

Then, without warning, a drill sergeant ordered us into a large hall and shouted,

"Undress trainees. Bag and tag those civilian clothes. Take everything off, now!"

We looked around and did as we were told. Naked and cold, we were then herded into a long line to be measured and issued our uniforms and boots. I started to voice my concerns about how poorly everything seemed to fit and was met with an immediate,

"This is not a fancy clothing store, Trainee! Take what we give you and make it work. Next!"

Everything, from our underwear and socks down to our toothbrush was government-issue—"G.I." for short. The message was clear—"You are now government property. Leave everything else behind. Is that understood, Trainee?"

After we received a barrage of vaccinations, a drill sergeant came screaming into the recovery room.

"What are you doing, Trainee? Who do you think you are?"

Uh oh, I thought, someone's in trouble, and looked around to see which poor fellow was in his sights. With a sharp turn, the sergeant continued barreling in our direction. His size wasn't all that imposing. But everyone in the room felt his intensity and anger, and cringed. This man has killed people, and here we are like sitting ducks.

"What's the meaning of this insubordination, Trainee?"

As he approached, I wondered why he was looking at me.

He exploded inches from my face.

"On your feet, Trainee. Now!" He was furious. "Don't you know you're not supposed to wear your hat inside the building?"

Well, I thought inwardly, no, not really. But what's the big deal, anyway? Why don't you just ask me to take it off? Outwardly, I froze and stood stiffly in agonizing silence.

"I ought to take you outside and show you what's good for you, Trainee," he bellowed, as fine bits of spit shot from his mouth and stuck to my forehead and nose.

We haven't even started our training yet. Or have we? I mused.

"Keep that hat off your head, and your head out of your ass, Trainee," he added.

Another eternity passed with the drill sergeant's hot face inches from mine, as the other recruits watched in silent dread.

"You better get your shit together, Trainee. Show some respect for the rules," he growled, as he turned and stormed from the room.

What rules? I thought. I haven't been told anything about wearing or not wearing hats inside. There's no sign. This whole army thing makes zero sense. How am I supposed to know what to do? And what's with all the damn yelling, anyway?

Then it dawned on me. We're not supposed to figure it out. Just do as we're told, just like the man said. I thought, this is what's happening, Larry, whether you like it or not.

The message is simple and unmistakable. Listen, learn what to do and when to do it, and do it. As simple as that.

"Sorry, Coach," was replaced with, "Yes, Drill Sergeant. Right away, Drill Sergeant!"

But I *chose* basketball, I argued internally. *This*, I most assuredly, did *not* choose. But clearly, my life is no longer in my own hands. So, what am I going to do about it? And if freedom is about having choices, what choices do I have in a situation as hopeless as this, anyway?

Henry's words came to mind. Something he said during my struggles with basketball in high school. "Always choose the light. Go with that, and it will lift you."

But where's the light in this God-forsaken place? I wondered. All these uniformed soldiers marching around day and night in lockstep formation. All the incessant hollering. The endless rows of identical barracks. The constant crack, crack, crack of rifles from the firing range. And those questionable smells wafting across the drill field from the mess hall.

This, I concluded, is a big mistake. I don't belong here. What happened to my dream of a brilliant, college basketball run? And what about getting a good education and making something of myself? All my dreams—up in smoke. And I've let my family down and all the others who believed in me. Most of all, I've let myself down.

As I felt my life disintegrating around me, I made a pledge: If I get out of this mess alive—and that's clearly not a given—I want my life to be my own. For better or worse, I decide. No more falling asleep at the wheel!

A week or so into basic training, we began the punishing daily ritual of early-morning maneuvers. Marching endlessly around the base, we huffed out rhythmic, gung-ho army chants, as our breath turned to steam in the frosty air. When I was certain my aching body couldn't take another step, we abruptly came to a halt in front of a training area containing a wide assortment of logs, walls, ropes, barbed wire, trenches, and mud pits.

"Come on, put some energy into it, Trainees," shouted our drill sergeants, as we scrambled onto the obstacle course and began a grueling round of battlefield simulation training, complete with live rounds exploding over our mud-covered helmets.

"Lower," they demanded. "Keep your head down, Trainee. You wanna get it shot off your shoulders?" Then it was "Higher. Get your ass over that wall, Trainee. Now!"

My body and mind begged for rest. And then, we suddenly stopped again.

"Line up, Trainees. Stand up straight. Shoulders back. Chin down. What are you looking at, Trainee? Face ahead."

One moment I was sweating profusely as I ran and crawled and climbed around the training ground. The next minute we were all told to stand at attention, shivering in the sub-freezing temperatures. Next, we were ordered to sit on a set of icy, cold, metal bleachers. As we huddled against the wind and blew into our hands, lunch was issued from the back of a large, green, flatbed truck.

"Oh man. Hot food," guys began to celebrate under their breath. "I'm so cold I could eat the whole damn truck full, just to get my body warmed up again." Our hot meal, however, was lazily slapped onto thin metal trays rendering everything ice cold by the time we sat to gulp it down.

"'Damn. You gotta be kidding me. This army shit is some kinda torture.'"

And for dessert, they served the whole company ice cream!

While I was wondering what might come next, a burly drill sergeant with a clipboard under his arm trudged out of a nearby tent and yelled,

"Can any of you morons type?"

It's so cold, I thought. What's this guy yelling about now? What he was shouting suddenly registered, and I looked up.

"What did he say?" I asked the guy sitting next to me. "Did he ask who can type?"

It was the 1960s. Men didn't type.

Thank you, big brother, I thought. The two of us had discussed the subject more than once, and Al Junior had absolutely insisted I take typing in high school. "It was the best course I took in high school," he had argued. And so, I had decided to take it. There had even been some nice girls in the class, too.

"Yes," I raised my hand and shouted with newfound hope, not knowing the actual implications of my answer, except for the possibility of getting out of the cold for a little while. "Yes, Drill Sergeant. I can type."

Out of a company of 200 trainees, only five of us raised our hands.

"Okay, you guys follow me," the drill sergeant demanded as he turned to leave. We followed him into his tent, mumbling to one another on the way. Inside were chairs and desks. On the top of each desk sat an ancient, army-green typewriter.

"Sit down at a desk, Trainees. You're taking a 5-minute test to see how fast you can type." He clicked the stopwatch hanging on the cord around his neck. "Start typing, Trainees. Now!" he ordered.

Five minutes later, it was, "Stop typing, Trainees! Get back to your platoon."

And off we went. Nothing more was said about the results of that test during the whole of basic training.

Our company of two hundred trainees had four fifty-man platoons. Each platoon was appointed a trainee leader who had the unique opportunity to gain leadership experience, army style. Trainee leaders were responsible for making sure all the guys in their platoon did everything right and learned the basic skills of marching, weapons handling, physical development, and cleanliness. Our current platoon leader was a thirty-year-old who had served a previous term of duty. His gap in service, however, meant he had to go through basic training again, and he was not thrilled about it.

Two weeks into basic training, one of our drill sergeants called us to attention and stood toe-to-toe with our leader.

"Trainee," he glared into the smaller man's face. "You are hereby relieved of your platoon leader duties."

A hush fell over the platoon. Uh oh, I thought, what does that mean?

"Private Holmes, you are now the new platoon leader," my drill sergeant announced gruffly in my direction. The muscles in my stomach tightened as I held my breath.

I must have heard that wrong, I surmised. I have purposefully been keeping a very low profile, just doing everything I was told to the best of my ability.

The drill sergeant moved down the line and stood in front of me.

This just gets worse, I thought, staring straight ahead and trying not to flinch. So much for blending in, not making mistakes, and not drawing any attention to myself. Clearly that was a failed strategy. And now, for some reason, he wants me to stand out front and lead the entire platoon.

How does this whole army thing work, anyway? Do I have a choice?

"Any questions, Trainee?" the drill sergeant leaned in and asked with a smirk.

I've never been in charge of anything, I argued to the universe. This is a big mistake.

"No, Drill Sergeant," I heard myself say. "I mean, what am I supposed to do?"

"You're supposed to do a good job, Trainee. Dismissed," was his reply.

Well, I thought, that's about as clear as mud. I guess I'm about to find out.

"Tomorrow morning, o-six-hundred-hours, Trainees," the drill sergeant yelled as we filed away from the training grounds at the end of the day. "Five-mile forced march in full combat gear. Be ready."

Five miles? Full combat gear? Uniform, combat boots, helmet, rifle, fifty-pound pack. This is going to be brutal. It should make for an interesting first day at work.

The helmets issued in basic training were from the Second World War and felt like we were strapping a cast-iron skillet to our head. Our weapons were also WW II-era M1 rifles. They were accurate, but again, very heavy. The combat boots, even when they fit, were so heavy and clumsy, it seemed they'd been specially designed to inhibit rather than facilitate any movement.

"Lights out early, men," I told my platoon at the end of the day. "Big day tomorrow." I had almost said, "Big game tomorrow."

Five a.m. came quickly, and we woke to more than a foot of snow. It was still coming down in giant floating waves as we set off into a freezing headwind at six. We struggled to lift our boots out of the growing drifts while keeping our top-heavy gear balanced on our heads and backs.

Several hours into the march, we heard, "Company halt!" from the drill sergeant at the head of the line.

Finally, I thought, looking to see how everyone was holding up, a break.

One of my guys looked pretty shaky on his feet, like he was dizzy or disoriented. As I turned to see if he was okay, he pitched forward like a tree trunk and landed face down in the knee-high snow.

Okay, I thought, as I walked over to see what was going on. This might be my responsibility to deal with this. He probably just needs a hand up.

"Trainee!" we heard thundering down the line, "you'd better get your sorry ass up, and quick, if you know what's good for you!" Our drill sergeant's tirade of venom continued uninterrupted as he bounded in our direction through the snow.

"Don't just lay there like a piece of shit!" he yelled, kicking snow at the backpack of the trainee buried beneath it. "Get your ass up, and I mean now, you good-for-nothing, son-of-a-bitch trainee! On your feet!" he spluttered and kicked the snow again.

"Drill Sergeant, what are you doing?" I heard coming out of my mouth, calm and steady as you please.

"He can't hear you, Drill Sergeant. He's unconscious," I added with no inflections.

The drill sergeant stopped his snow kicking and turned his rage in my direction. I looked him in the eye, swallowed, and said as calmly and clearly as I could,

"We will take care of our own, Drill Sergeant."

The magnitude of the moment came into sharper focus. Oh no! was the first thought going through my mind. This is bad. This is really bad. Whatever's going to happen next cannot be good.

I and one hundred and ninety-eight other guys waited in fear and disbelief for what would surely be a swift and devastating response from the drill sergeant. His cold stare lingered in the wintry air like a specter. Trainee number two-hundred remained face-down in the snow.

"You just make sure you take care of him, then, trainee platoon leader," he said, without blinking, "and the rest of your men too." Then he turned and walked away.

A shocked and dumbfounded silence fell over our company like a soft and oddly comforting blanket of snow.

"What just happened?" was all I could think and feel. My surprising words, and his, reverberated long afterward, and we all knew something had changed.

Over the next few days, it felt odd, and a bit uncomfortable, as I began to realize my fellow platoon members were looking to me for guidance and direction. Unlike my announced appointment as trainee platoon leader, an unspoken shift had occurred. We had all witnessed what I did and said to the drill sergeant. And it wasn't going away.

Everyone in the army, even trainees, know that speaking disrespectfully to a superior officer is a clear and unforgivable violation of the military's strict code of conduct and can lead to court-martial and even military imprisonment. Yet subconsciously, I had chosen to ignore the code. Where did that impulse come from, I wondered, as I awaited my fate over the coming days.

"Trainee, come with me to my office. I want to talk to you," the drill sergeant said the following week.

Oh, well, I thought, this is it, then. He's going to lay it all on me now.

"Do you understand what happened between us the other day, Trainee?" he asked when we entered his office and he shut the door. "Do you understand why I didn't punish you for your disrespectful behavior?"

"No, not really, Sergeant," I answered truthfully.

"It was because I believed you weren't being deliberately insubordinate, or stupid, for that matter. What I believed I was seeing was a soldier who was willing, perhaps somewhat foolishly, to stand up for his men no matter what the cost to him personally. That, Trainee, is a quality we want to draw out. I was never going to punish you for that."

He stopped to make sure it was sinking in and then continued.

"Everything we do here is meant to build combat skills and obedience to the chain of command. It's also meant to create a feeling of camaraderie and a spirit of teamwork. I believe you stumbled onto some potential for leadership in yourself, Trainee. You may have been surprised to find you have some form of courage in yourself, am I right?" he asked, and then he leaned toward me and, to my great surprise, laughed out loud.

"In a combat situation, you never know what's going to happen. Luck or destiny play a big part, but training is what can prepare you for anything."

As he sat himself down, he nodded toward the chair facing his desk, indicating I was also to sit.

"On one of my tours of duty in Vietnam, my platoon was on patrol out in the jungle, and I got separated from the others. I figured I could find my way back to them. I turned a corner and came face to face with the enemy, a fierce-looking, little Vietcong soldier. We were so close I could smell the garlic and fish sauce on his breath. He tried to fire, but his weapon jammed. I fired my rifle. Point blank. I couldn't miss him."

He lowered his voice and continued more slowly,

"My training meant I didn't panic. When his weapon jammed, I didn't think, I just responded."

Nope, I thought. I can't really imagine being in some jungle fighting for my life. And I'm not so sure I could shoot another person, at point-blank range, even if my life depended on it.

"All of this training," the drill sergeant continued, "may seem harsh, or meaningless, or even unnecessary right now. But it's for a purpose. One day, it may save your life, or the lives of men you're leading. You're dismissed, Trainee." With that he nodded his head toward the door and turned to a stack of paper on his desk.

During our first month of basic training, we weren't allowed to leave the base. Not even on weekends when there was no training. We weren't even allowed to leave our immediate company area—basically the barracks and mess hall.

There were, however, small pizza trucks that came to all the barracks. But, under the threat of severe punishment, we were not allowed to go downstairs to order anything from them.

"Man, smell that pizza. It's driving me crazy. I gotta have some," guys started complaining. "Three floors up, and that smell is killing me."

"Yes," we all agreed. "Especially after three weeks of food from the mess hall."

This went on for several days. Then someone suggested, "Let's tie sheets together with a pillowcase at the end and put our order and money inside."

Others chimed in, "Yeah, yeah! The guy can put our pizzas in the pillowcases, and we can pull them back up." Our collective agreement was reinforced with cries of

"Execute the strategy. Achieve the objective. Take the hill. Take no prisoners."

Inwardly, I thought this could all go horribly wrong, and I'm supposed to be in charge. But the energy of the moment was more powerful. We lowered our string of sheets and yelled down to the driver,

"Hey, we've got a big order coming your way!" The pizza guy looked around. We shouted again, he looked up, and we pointed to our pillowcase delivery system.

We had gathered good intel and provided him with exact change. He read our note, gave us the thumbs up, took our money, and stuffed our pizzas inside. We yanked them up to the third floor to cheers of "Mission accomplished!"

It was, perhaps, our most significant experience of team building in all of basic training. And we didn't get caught!

Thousands of young men like me were being trained to fight. However, the greater purpose and outcome of the war itself was being called into question by a growing number of Americans and others around the world, especially young people, who took part in antiwar protests and marches on college campuses across the country throughout the war's duration.

Villages in Vietnam were being bombed, huge swathes of jungle defoliated or incinerated, children and families were sometimes the victims, in dreadful missions gone wrong. The stories and images on national television and in magazines and newspapers were horrifying and brought the brutality of war agonizingly close to home.

As a draftee, the feeling of having no choice was the hardest thing to stomach. How is all this going to play out? I wondered. For us GIs? For our families? For our country? And the one question none of us wanted to ask out loud: When are we headed to the jungles of Vietnam?

In the barracks, many of us were debating the sense of it all. "Why do we have to be here? What's this war even about anyway?" Some guys argued, "Man, we got to protect our country and stand up for democracy. Or communism will be on our doorsteps." But all of us worried about what the future might bring for us. We hung out together in the evenings, drinking, smoking joints, and talking long into the night about our predicament. Stronger substances were available too.

"Hey, dude, try some of this shit. You'll be in another universe, man."

"Any place would be better than this one."

On the last day of basic training, we all stood around craning our necks to get a glimpse of the MOS (Military Occupational Specialty) assignment list posted outside barracks. Each of us was hoping to find one thing—anything other than AIT next to our name. AIT stood for Advanced Infantry Training, the code words for foot soldiers, or grunts. It meant there was only one place we were headed—to the jungles of Vietnam.

One by one, I saw the look of sadness and even despair unfold on the faces of my fellow trainees when they discovered their fate. Then I found my name and saw Personnel Management Specialist Training next to my name.

What's this? I wondered. I'm down for Personnel Training? Surprise, excitement, and relief welled up inside me all at once. But that's, well, that's fantastic.

I wanted to jump up and down and shout for joy. Then I looked around again at all the guys trying to take in their bad news and make some sense of it. "God help us, we're going to 'Nam."

What did our drill sergeant say to me in his office? "You never know what's going to happen. Luck or destiny play a big part in it."

But why, I wondered, do I get to stay stateside, while so many of my friends are going off to fight? And then I remembered, "Can any of you morons type?"

Another ray of light. Thank you, Al Junior. I might just owe you my life.

I phoned home to tell Mom and Dad about the graduation ceremony at the end of basic training, and they answered in unison, "We'll be there, son." It wasn't the college graduation ceremony I'd envisioned, but my parents and siblings seemed proud of me just the same, and all of us were relieved my next training was in personnel, not infantry. Years later, in a conversation with my younger brother, Ralph, he described the way my dad responded when I left for basic training.

"Dad was really upset when you got drafted, Larry. He didn't understand what had gone so wrong at college, and he worried a lot about what might happen to you in the army."

Huh, I thought, could have fooled me.

After basic training, I continued another eight weeks on the same base at Fort Dix in New Jersey. Then I was sent to Advanced Personnel Management Training at Fort Benjamin Harrison in Indiana. For a solid month, every day, and for me, night as well, we studied the military rules and regulations that determine everything that goes on in the army and how to account for each soldier's activities, assignments, status, rank, and projected movements. For me, knowing how it all worked was important. Army regulations, I soon discovered, are very detailed and quite complex. But it also began to dawn on me that we were learning how the whole system worked, from the inside out. The knowledge I gained was very empowering, and I was increasingly motivated to learn as much as I could.

The army was tough, demanding, and in your face. On the other hand, my time in training also felt like a kind of awakening to what I was capable of. Instead of struggling through the laws of physics and their esoteric applications, I began to realize, I'm actually starting to get a handle on who I am by dealing with real life situations. For all its many faults, the continuously demanding scenarios the army insisted we face during basic training and beyond required us to have clarity about our purpose and intent, followed by a precise set of responses and actions. And the results of those actions seemed instantaneous. The learning for me: Good strategies lead to likely success. Bad ones to failure.

The Vietnam war was a confusing and polarizing conflict. At the end of basic training, everyone was excited to finally be allowed off base on weekends. As a newly minted soldier, called to serve our country, I naively imagined receiving nods of respect from my fellow citizens when I walked around town in my uniform, especially after what I'd already endured just in basic training. I was sorely mistaken. On my first trip home, I walked into the airport and was met with nothing but sullen glances and suspicious stares. As I walked past a young couple, one of them said under her breath, "Why are you fighting in Vietnam? Are you a baby killer, too?"

In those days, being black almost naturally came with a sense of second-class citizenship in America. I'd learned to live with that. But these comments and looks were a surprise and struck me even more deeply.

5

TAKE THE CONTROLS!

I'd figured my time in the army would be two years of living hell, and honestly, I was just hoping I would live through it. Instead, I felt like I'd reached a major turning point in my life.

Advanced training in Indianapolis ended. I was assigned permanent duty as personnel management specialist in charge of administrative duties at Fort Wolters just outside a little town called Mineral Wells, Texas—wherever that was. I grew up on cowboy movies and TV westerns, but nothing could have prepared me for the dry, dusty, rolling plains of north-central Texas.

The military function of the base was to provide the first twenty weeks of training for young, aspiring helicopter pilots destined to serve in Vietnam. To qualify for this training, young men had to enlist for a minimum of three years and be willing, without *any* doubts, to face a very dangerous battlefield assignment. This was not a place for the weak of heart. It was for the bravest of the brave.

When I arrived, two sizable staff members escorted me into the mess hall, offered me coffee, ordered me to sit, and provided a short overview of the base.

"Welcome to Camp Wolters," one of them began, raising his voice over the piercing whir and whup-whup-whup of helicopter blades just outside the mess hall window. "First, we're gonna go over what we call the 'Three 'F's.' That's the 'Facts, Functions, and Facilities' of this base," he said, in a kind of shout.

Tour guide number two took this as his cue, pulled on both ends of a telescoping metal pointer, and began tapping on a series of posters showing the various types of helicopters used on the base for training purposes. At the top of each poster was written in three-inch letters: "Types of Helicopters Currently Available for Training Purposes at Fort Wolters."

"These *here*," he shouted over the din of whooshing blades, while pointing to several photos on each poster, "*these* are the birds currently available to us for training purposes here at Fort Wolters."

Got it, I thought, nodding attentively.

"And this 'un *here*," he bellowed, undaunted by the constant lifting and dropping of helicopters behind him, "this *here* is the goal of every damn trainee pilot on this base."

Using his shiny pointer he proudly drew my attention to the large photo of a single, menacing helicopter in the middle of one poster, with grim-looking men in full combat gear jumping out of it.

"This one here is the army's newly upgraded UH-1 Huey Cobra helicopter. It's the workhorse of this war, and it's a damn powerful and very agile fighting machine."

"'Cuz they don't need no runway to take off or to land," tour guide number one eagerly interjected and then demonstrated, raising both hands up quickly, palms down, and slowly lowering them back down. "And they can carry a whole shitload of fully armed troops into and out of combat zones…"

"And protect their asses while they're doing it," number two continued, earnestly. "And let me tell you, these babies have saved a ton of our boys' lives. And it's *our* pilots who trained here at Fort Wolters, that are flyin' 'em in and out of those shit-hole jungles over there."

With that, tour guide number two turned to number one and nodded his approval.

"That's the end of our presentation," tour guide one yelled, looking in my general direction for the first time. Now we'll take a little drive around base, point a few things out, and take you to your new quarters."

"Sounds good" I said, standing. "Thank you."

These guys had apparently given this tour on more than one occasion, and they clearly loved their work, but what in God's name, I thought, am I doing here? This place is obviously an extremely important part of the war effort, and now here I am right in the middle of the whole damn mess. On the other hand, I thought, I'm not in Vietnam. At least not yet.

My twosome of over-sized guides took me on a quick tour around the base and dropped me off in front of a long, two-story structure and pointed me toward the personnel office at the far end on the ground floor. As I entered the barracks, I noticed a sizable gap between the bottom of the door and the floor and thought to myself, aren't there a lot of snakes and scorpions in Texas? I hoped that wouldn't create any problems.

At the end of a long, cavernous hallway, I found a compact office laden with stacks and piles of papers and files on every horizontal surface. Every desk. The top of every filing cabinet. And covering a lion's share of the floor.

Oh boy, this is bad, I thought. There didn't seem to be any order to it. In fact, it was not at all like the filing system I was taught in Indianapolis. And the internal systems might not be completely organized either.

A guy leaned into view from behind one of the stacks on the desk and said in a perky kind of voice, "Hey, you must be the new personnel specialist."

"That's me," I said. "This looks like quite—a big job you're doing here."

"Oh yeah, well, I don't really have any training for this assignment," he replied with a sigh and a quick roll of his eyes. "On the other hand," he added with a shrug, "I've taught myself as best I could. You know, learning on the job. So, I can show you what's in all these piles before my term of service ends. Then I'm a free man again." "Yee-ha-a-w," he added, pumping his fists over his head with a sheepish grin.

Nope, this is not good, I thought. Not good at all. My mind launched into various critical and blaming kinds of thoughts about all of the time and effort it would take me to clean up this crazy mess and get the place in order. I started getting a sinking, in-over-my-head kind of feeling in my gut. How in the world, I wondered, will I ever sort through all this and get it all organized? This could take forever!

Over the next few weeks, my fellow specialist talked me through his "system," explaining the purpose of each pile, what was in them, and the general reasoning behind his various decisions—uninformed as they were by any inkling of Army regulations.

It's like trying to unravel a ball of string, was the kindest thought I could muster.

All day, every day, for two weeks, the two of us worked in that small office until dinner. After dinner, we worked two or three more hours. Top-priority stacks and piles became sorted enough to enable me to assess the situation. Fixing it was another kettle of fish and would come later.

During our countless hours together, the incessant sound of helicopters taking off, hovering, and landing was the familiar background music of our common labors. And every now and then there was an unusually loud sound of something crashing.

"What's going on out there?" I asked one evening, over the whoosh of chopper blades and screaming sirens.

"Could be a crash. Every now and then that happens too. There's no completely risk-free way of teaching them how to fight in a war."

And this is just training, I thought.

"This must be what it feels like to be in a war zone," I said. "Never being far enough away to completely relax. But it's so dark out there. How can they possibly still be flying this late?"

"Oh," he answered, looking up from the stacks of paper on his side of the desk, "that's called night flying. They have to master that skill to be prepared for their twenty-four-seven job in Vietnam. There aren't *any* off hours in a combat zone."

Okay, I concluded, with a welcome sense of relief, what's so hard about what we're doing here in this little office? We're safe, well-fed (sort of), have a roof over our heads, and best of all, we're not being shot at...or crashing helicopters that we're trying to learn how to fly.

Along with this newly emerging point of view came a critical insight and decision on my part. Applying my training as a personnel specialist isn't much of a sacrifice, and it's certainly not dangerous. So, why not do it as best I can? Accepting this challenge actually felt like the right thing to do here.

"Are they paying you or are you working for free?" I could hear my dad ask in my head. This is what he often asked when one of us kids complained about an unfair situation at work.

"Yeah, they're paying me," was the typical answer.

"Well then," he'd say with a twinkle in his eye, "your job is simple. You just do the best you can do. Forget all that other nonsense."

Helpful input, I guess, though at the time I'm pretty sure we were hoping more for empathy than sage advice. But if the shoe fits…, I thought, and in this case, the army is paying me. And they actually trained me to do this job right here in front of me. It's up to me. If I genuinely want to do my best, which I do, I better roll up my sleeves and get busy.

After the other specialist finished his time, I continued to work twelve-hour days. The first sergeant in charge of all the enlisted men in the company came into my office after work one day. He was a career soldier from Guam—immaculate in his uniform, short, stout, with an ever-firm look on his face. First sergeants are known for having high standards and being fiercely demanding of their men.

Uh, oh, I thought. I wonder what he wants?

"Specialist Holmes," he said. "You're still here?"

"Yes, Top," I said, looking around at the various piles waiting for me to tackle. "I've got a bit to do to get all this straightened out and put in working order."

"Top" is an army expression for the highest-ranking, non-commissioned officer or first sergeant.

"Yes, yes," he nodded, as his face opened into a broad approving smile, "the other specialist worked hard, but he clearly wasn't trained to do the job. Keep up the work." He turned and left.

A couple of weeks later he came into my office again.

"Hey, Specialist Holmes, it's starting to look good in here. Is everything in order?"

"Well," I said, "it's getting there, Top. I'm doing my best, but it's slow work to get it really in tip-top shape."

He seemed deep in thought as he looked around the office. He didn't speak for a good half a minute, and when he did, his words were measured and direct.

"Just do what you need to do here. Don't worry about having to do anything else."

"Yes, Top," I said.

But as he turned to leave, his look suggested he wasn't quite sure if I really understood the full meaning of what he had said. I reflected on his words and their possible meanings. My first thought was about mandatory roll call at six a.m. every morning. Yuck! Outside in every imaginable kind of weather, everybody assembles, and the company leader yells, "Report." Each platoon leader yells, "All present and accounted for, Sir." Then we all scuttle back into the barracks for two hours and report for duty at eight a.m. sharp. That's the drill.

This annoying military tradition, like most, comes from the wartime need to make sure every soldier is present and accounted for. But in this particular situation here, I reasoned, crack-of-dawn roll call is a major pain in my ass. Plus, every few weeks there's some "extra duty" assignment thrown in for good measure—kitchen police, patrol, mess hall—yet more pains in the ass.

As if he'd been reading my mind, the first sergeant grinned and quipped,

"Specialist Holmes, you don't have to do roll call or any of that extra duty stuff. You're working plenty hard. You're my man."

I blinked. I wasn't sure I believed what I was hearing.

"Okay, Top," was the only thing that came to mind. I am definitely cool with that, I thought. Over the coming weeks, I continued my slow but steady climb toward getting the base's administrative systems in good shape.

At 8:00 a.m., the first sergeant walked punctually through my office door, as this had become his first-thing-in-the-morning custom.

"Good morning, Specialist. Good news. You don't have to worry. You're not going anywhere."

Simple words. But fully pregnant with implications. Smiling from ear to ear, he started patting me on the back with his forearm, like it was almost half of a hug. First Sergeant's personality matched his low-to-the-ground, muscular build. Straightforward. No-frills. A no-nonsense, in-your-face kind of guy. He meant what he said and said what he meant.

"Specialist Holmes," he beamed, "what you're doing with all our administrative systems reflects very positively on me, and more importantly, on our commanding officer. From that perspective, this company is looking good. In fact, quite good."

I knew exactly what he meant, this time. What I'd sensed was now confirmed. I'M NOT GOING TO VIETNAM! My heart started pounding in my chest. This is good. This is huge. What an amazing relief—for me, and for my whole family! I lowered my gaze and thought, I'm glad such amazingly good news is coming from my first sergeant. This guy has really had my back. This whole time he's been teaching me, and encouraging me, and looking out for me. This is the light Henry's on about.

"Okay, Top," I mustered, with a grin of my own. "That's some very good news. Thank you."

A new, high-ranking, strictly-by-the-books kind of sergeant came crashing into our company a few weeks later. He was a grade below our first sergeant in rank. But he was significantly taller, more imposing physically, and was more than eager to issue instructions about every possible topic he could think of.

"Soldier," he screamed one morning, tearing into one of the guys trying to get dressed, "you better clean up this mess, and straighten up your uniform!" The guy looked around to see if anyone understood what exactly he was meant to do, since he only had about half of his uniform on. The impressively sized sergeant turned sharply on his heel, pointed in the general direction of the hallway, and shouted to no one in particular,

"Who's in charge of this space? Answer me that!" More sideway glances from all of us.

A few days into our newest sergeant's tenure on base, he took it upon himself to make sure everyone was out of bed and outside for roll call each morning. The bugle blew, and I caught some vague rumblings of guys getting up and ready. I pulled the covers over my head and happily closed my eyes.

"Soldier," the giant growled, as he flung open my door and stormed into my room, "get your sorry ass out of bed. It's time for roll call. Now!"

Fear and doubt arose for an instant, as I struggled to frame an appropriate response to the predicament. Ah yes, I recalled with relief, Top's got my back on this. I gathered my courage and politely informed him,

"I don't actually do roll calls, Sergeant."

"Soldier," he shot back as his face reddened directly in front of mine, "EVERYONE does roll call in this man's army. Get your ass up, RIGHT NOW, and report!"

"I don't, Sergeant," I repeated.

Now he was getting seriously angry.

What's going to happen now? I wondered.

"This is insubordination, Soldier!" he shouted. "I'm reporting you to the first sergeant. Then we'll see what tune you're playing."

"Just a second, Sergeant," I said, as he turned to leave.

He pivoted around. "Change of heart, Soldier?"

"No, Sergeant," I offered gingerly, but with a cheeky feeling of satisfaction too, "could you please close the door behind you?"

An explosion of slamming doors, foul language, and stomping feet thundered down the hallway in the direction of the first sergeant's office. I pulled the covers over my head and burst out laughing. I considered the possible fallout from my actions—or lack thereof—but quickly concluded it was better to get some more sleep for the long day ahead. I had stood my ground. That was fun. It felt good and right, come what may.

On the way to my office later, I passed the first sergeant's office, and he waved me in.

"Hey, Specialist," he said in a low and concerned tone, "what happened with you and that nice, new sergeant of ours this morning? Man, oh man, he was really hot. I told him not to worry, I'd take care of it for him. That seemed to calm him down a bit."

Top broke up laughing. We both laughed.

A few days passed, and there were no more early morning altercations.

"What's up with that new sergeant, Top?" I asked the first sergeant. "I haven't seen him around lately."

"Oh yeah," he grinned, "that guy had to leave. Told me our post isn't disciplined enough for him."

Fort Wolters, Texas, wasn't a combat zone. But still, a helicopter training school isn't the safest place to be. Learning to fly a helicopter is incredibly demanding, both physically and mentally. Almost every other day, the sirens started blaring, indicating something serious had happened —usually another helicopter crash. Trainees sustained injuries sometimes. Occasionally there were fatalities.

The system and the training pilots, in truth, were really good at what they did. Regardless, on a regular basis, I looked out the window of my office to see smoke rising from the latest incident and wondered how serious it was.

Part of my personnel role was to record each incident in a file—what the army called the "Morning Report." Before each crash, most of the trainees were just a name to me. Afterward though—especially with injuries—the gravity of the situation became more apparent, and I thought, this man is a real, flesh-and-blood human being.

I looked into their records and saw their ages—some as young as eighteen. I saw where they were from and wondered what kind of family and community they each grew up in. Stories formed in my mind—a quaint little hometown, parents and siblings seeing them off, the size of their high school graduation class. What will his friends and family think when they hear he's been injured, and just in training?

We got a new lieutenant assigned to an administrative position in our company upon his return from a tour of duty in Vietnam. As they often say in the army, everyone has to have a role. The rub comes when you're a combat troop or officer trained in battle tactics and fighting, and you return from the battlefield. What's an appropriate stateside assignment for someone who's seen that kind of action?

Lieutenant Bates was a regular, fun-loving, down-to-earth guy in his mid-twenties, and it soon became apparent he knew little or nothing about the administrative details he was assigned to oversee. He walked into my office his first morning on duty.

"Well, Specialist," he said, with a bemused kind of smirk, "I really don't have a clue about any of this admin stuff. So, how are we going to handle this situation?"

"No worries, Lieutenant," I replied. "I've got this under control. Just ask me whatever you need to know, and I'll get it done for you."

"Ah," he beamed, "we're going to make a great team."

What Lieutenant Bates didn't know about admin was generously out-weighed by what he did know about combat. One of his closest buddies—a younger warrant officer and helicopter instructor pilot who had also just returned from Vietnam—loved to hang out in my office, shoot the breeze, and share stories with Lieutenant Bates. In my very *small* office!

Late one afternoon, the lieutenant left the room, and his buddy leaned toward me, lowered his voice, and asked,

"You know he's a war hero, don't you?"

"No," I answered, raising my eyebrows, "I don't."

He looked out into the hallway and listened for the lieutenant's return.

"He doesn't like me telling this story," he whispered, "but once the platoon he went out to rescue was being hit hard by a surprise attack from the Vietcong. They'd dug this giant, underground network of tunnels and used it to ambush our troops. They attacked, and then they just vanished into their tunnels. Vietnamese people are pretty small compared to most Americans, and their tunnels are usually too tight for our guys to get into and move around in. Most of our combat troops just plain refuse to even try.

"So, Lieutenant Bates flies out to evacuate our guys, but they're all pinned down by the enemy combatants, and none of 'em can even get to his chopper. So, what does he do? He gets so pissed-off, he lands his damn helicopter, takes out his pistol, runs over, and crams his big old ass into one of those little tunnels, and then he proceeds to clear out all of those Vietcong—like it's all in a day's work."

He leaned back in his chair, folded his arms, and added, "Don't ask for more details. Anyways, he's a hero."

Lieutenant Bates walked in, looked at our faces, and asked, "What's up?"

"Nothing," his buddy answered. "Not a damn thing, Lieutenant."

The instructor pilot's story made me wonder what the lieutenant was like before he joined the army. How was he able to call on such a combative and violent side of himself and still be such a nice, down-to-earth kind of guy? And what motivates someone like him to even perform such acts of bravery?

"The training prepares you," I heard my old drill sergeant say in my head. "This training prepares you to function and survive the extreme situations of war."

But no one forced helicopter pilots to sign up for this assignment. Going in, they had to have known it was more than likely they'd eventually be injured in the course of their service. And that the odds of helicopter pilots returning unscathed, physically or emotionally, from a tour of duty in Vietnam were slim.

This, I surmised, is a testament to the strength and depth of their patriotism—to serve their country in this way.

In my heart, though, I also knew combat and war were not where I wanted to be. But where I was being called wasn't clear to me. I wanted to serve my community in some meaningful and helpful way. This I knew. But how all this military experience and training would prepare me for that remained a mystery.

Lieutenant Bates and his warrant officer buddy came into my office early one morning as usual—to hang out, drink coffee, and shoot the breeze. The lieutenant sat down in his favorite chair, leaned back, and kicked his feet up on my desk in a single, flowing motion. His younger sidekick, on the other hand, sat down rather gingerly, and seemed to wince a bit in the process.

Bates laughed when he saw I'd noticed this and turned in my direction, cupping the back of his hand to the side of his mouth.

"He's got a delicacy issue," he said, pretending to whisper.

"What's that?" I asked.

"He got shot in his ass."

"Oh no. Really? How'd it happen?"

"Well," Lieutenant Bates said, looking out the corner of his eyes at his friend, "our ace pilot here was doing a pick-up and evac under some pretty heavy enemy fire. He managed to land and get his troops on board, but when he took off, he copped a bullet right in his buttocks. The thing is, Specialist Holmes," he paused for effect, "the weakest part of a Huey Cobra is the underbelly—where the armor's thinnest. Coming in, those birds are fierce—rockets firing, door gunners blazing away. Everyone down below runs for cover. But when you're taking off, you can't fire your rockets, and the door gunners have a hard time getting their firing angle right. Taking off under fire in a Huey, you're a sitting duck. And that, my friends, is exactly when the terrible deed was done." He cracked up laughing and the red-faced warrant officer shrugged with a sheepish grin.

This kind of teasing felt familiar, like locker room banter after a basketball game. But despite the sprinkling of humor, their stories were of shocking violence and death. Chalk it up to the brashness of youth? Or to their need for emotional release after surviving such extreme danger? I hadn't fought in a war, so what did I know? On the other hand, I didn't really want to know.

I was conflicted. Here we were, a bunch of guys thrown together—from all different places, racial and economic backgrounds, and political persuasions—some by choice, others by fate. Regardless of our differences, there was a camaraderie and deep respect I felt for these two brave soldiers, just hanging out in my tiny little office. We were on the same team—fellow Americans serving our country. At least that's what I felt and believed. We had some sense of purpose. That's what kept us going each day.

As I started to get everything squared away in my office, I was able to reduce my twelve- to fourteen-hour workdays down to a more reasonable seven or eight hours. Okay, I thought, enough with sitting behind a desk all day. I need to get back into shape.

I knocked off early one afternoon and walking past the first sergeant's office asked, "Hey, Top, do you happen to know if there's a basketball court I could play on?"

"Oh, yeah," he said, looking up from a sizable stack of forms on his desk, "there's a gym on base just a couple-hundred yards from here. It's open most of the time, and anyone can use it."

"Cool," I said, "Thanks, Top," and eagerly headed out to change clothes and shoes and check things out. I was getting excited now.

I found the gym open and empty, and slipped easily into the familiar rhythm of "shooting around." As my body relaxed, I felt my heart grow light and joyful. Ah yes, I thought, this is more like it. This is my safe haven.

It felt great to get back out on the smooth, wooden floor, and it was exhilarating to watch my army-hardened body perform so well, despite my forced time away from the game. After an hour or so of pure enjoyment, I heard the gym doors swing open with a high-pitched squeak and quickly swing closed again with an extended kind of low-pitched grumble. I turned to see a guy wave and start to bounce a ball in my direction.

"Hi," he said in a friendly, self-assured manner, "looks like you've played quite a bit of ball. Where'd you play?"

"Oh, thanks," I answered, shaking his hand, "I'm Larry, by the way. I played for Fairleigh Dickinson for a couple of years."

"Cool, I'm Chris," he responded. "I played for the Buckeyes."

"Whoa. Ohio State! That's a good school" I said. "They've got some great teams." I was impressed. "You wanna shoot together? I'll rebound for you first."

We shot around together for an hour or so and then found ourselves talking about everything basketball, elated to find another soul with an equally deep knowledge of and love for "the game."

"Hey, you know what would be really great?" Chris asked with enthusiasm.

"What's that?" I asked.

"We should put a team together," he announced.

"What do you mean?" I asked, hopefully.

"Well," he answered, "last year we had a team that played in the local league, which is pretty good. Mostly guys that played in high school, and a few who played in college.

We got good enough to enter a team into the Fifth Army Tournament, which was some stiff competition. A lot more of those guys had played college ball."

Now I was really getting excited.

"Can we get the team back together?" I asked, thinking of the possibilities.

"Well, that's the thing," Chris warned, "there's this war going on, so most trainee pilots move in and out of here on a regular basis. It's hard to keep a team together."

"What about all the support troops on base?" I asked. "There's a lot more cooks, MPs, mechanics, and guys like me in admin than there are trainee pilots."

"Good point," he said. "Hopefully, if we dig deep enough, we can find some good players. Plus, I know a few guys that are still around from last year."

"Cool," I said. "Oh, and we'll need to find someone who can coach us, right?"

"You're plenty good enough, Larry" he suggested, without hesitation. "You can be our coach and play too."

Huh, I thought, here it is again, me being asked to step up, enter the ring, and grow my potential as a leader. Though I had to admit, this time around, I felt oddly eager to take on the challenge.

"You think so?" I asked, a bit lifted by the notion.

"Oh, yeah, man," he answered with a grin. "You'd be great. It's a no-brainer."

"Okay," I said. "Let's do it. I'll coach and play."

So, that was settled. Over the next few weeks, Chris and I started asking around and inviting guys to informal pick-up games. Eventually we had a good enough core group willing and able to commit, to form a team and start playing and practicing on a regular basis. Pretty soon we were playing in the local league, off-base in Mineral Wells. By the end of the season, we participated in the highly competitive Fifth Army's Southwest Regional Tournament, a huge accomplishment. Plus, we played well.

Getting back up on the horse again was invigorating and affirming for me, and I loved it. Everything I thought I'd lost when I was drafted had now manifested in an unexpected and rather remarkable form. Here I was, out on the floor, leading our guys through the drills Coach Ernst had so skillfully taught me, helping to build their physical strength and mental acuity, training them to think and play together as a team. We were competing at a high level against some really good players and having great fun doing it. I had somehow realized my dream. This is what I'd been looking for all along.

Several instructor pilots offered me a ride in their chopper during my time at the helicopter flight school in Mineral Wells, Texas. My unwavering response to each was always the same, "No, thank you. I'm not good with heights." This remained the case until the offer came from Lieutenant Bates.

"Specialist Holmes," he began, sitting with his feet up on my desk while I was working on some administrative reports one day, "you wanna come for a ride with me in a helicopter?"

"Sure," I heard myself say, followed by an immediate feeling of alarm in the pit of my stomach. What, I thought, have you just done, Larry? And then I considered the facts before me. Beyond a doubt, Lieutenant Bates knows what he's doing. I'll be safe. Who knows, maybe I'll even have some fun.

"Follow me, young man," the Lieutenant cocked his head with a grin. And out we went, right then and there, to the flight range.

"Here she is," offered the Lieutenant, with his arms out-stretched, as we walked up to the aircraft. "Ain't she a beaut'?"

This *cannot* be right, I thought.

"Climb on in, son, and buckle up," said the Lieutenant, briskly.

This was clearly not the Huey Cobra I'd somehow expected. In fact, it didn't look "fierce" in any way. He saw the look of doubt on my face, patted me on the back, and added,

"She's a good one, Specialist. An OH-23. We call 'em Ravens. 'Cause they're so scrappy."

Yes, I thought, that's a good word, "scrappy." Like a scrappy little—mosquito!

The contraption in front of us looked hardly big enough to fit two people shoulder to shoulder. Its body consisted of a modest, see-through, plastic bubble containing two seats, a surprisingly dinky-looking engine in the back, and a handful of dials, buttons, pedals, and levers in the front. A small opening was provided for getting in and out of each side of the bubble. But there was no door you could close. The bubble sat on two small metal skids, fashioned from what looked like thin pipes welded together. A modest tailpiece, also made of little pipes, stuck out the back, with a whirligig stuck on the end. Once we were seated, the lieutenant showed me how to buckle in, started the engine, and brought a thin little set of sagging blades to life with a shudder and a great, swooshing wall of air blasting into our bubble's holes from a very few, precious inches above our heads.

The lieutenant glanced in my direction.

"I have to keep my flight hours up," he explained over the din of whirling rotors, "to, you know, maintain my flight status."

I understood his need but sensed an ulterior motive.

"Hold on," he announced with glee, as the tiny bubble lifted slightly, skidded forward, gathered speed, and shot skyward like an elevator blasting out of its shaft. Left somewhere far below was my stomach.

Lieutenant Bates banked hard right without warning, laying us nearly on our side and underscoring my life's complete dependence on the seat belt keeping me from falling out of the hole on my side of the bubble. As we leveled out and smoothly continued to climb—considerably higher than I'd imagined such a scrappy little bird could go —I began to relax and even enjoy the widening scene below.

"You want to have a go?" the lieutenant asked without blinking.

He's got to be kidding, I thought, doesn't he?

"Ha, no. But thanks for the offer, Lieutenant," I said, with what I hoped was a nonchalant shrug of my shoulders.

I'd been serving at the helicopter training school long enough to have heard my share of harrowing stories about choppers. Starting with the generally accepted fact that they are considerably more difficult to fly than fixed-wing aircraft. For one thing, they don't glide. In other words—if the motor stalls, they go down—fast.

"Oh, come on, Specialist, give it a go," he prompted with his familiar grin

I didn't budge. I could barely breathe.

"Take the controls, Specialist Holmes," he commanded smoothly. With that, he unceremoniously took his hands off the controls, calmly leaned back in his seat, folded his arms, and nodded his head toward the lonely controls in front of me.

"What the...," I stammered. "No, I'm good!"

But there he sat, with a kind of bemused look on his face, and out of pure fear, I grabbed the two controls on my side of the bubble.

"That's right, Specialist," he said calmly. "That one there is for speed—what we call thrust. The other one positions the chopper blades to control your pitch—by easing forward or back on the stick. It controls your direction too —left or right on your stick. Give it a go—take us up and to the right—that's slowly forward and slowly to the right on your stick—nice and easy does it."

"I can't do this," I pleaded. "I don't think I can do this, Lieutenant."

"You're doing just fine, Specialist Holmes," he offered gently. "Just follow my instructions. Concentrate on the task at hand."

Okay, I found myself thinking, as the initial sense of panic subsided. Whoa! I'm actually doing this. I'm flying a helicopter! I was completely surprised and even elated.

A quarter of an hour into my flying lesson, Lieutenant Bates took over the controls, returned to base, and landed the chopper. On the ground, shaking, but energized, I told him,

"When you gave me those controls like that, I was terrified. I didn't have a clue what I was doing. Weren't you worried we would crash?"

He looked at me and smiled.

"I was teaching you how to pilot the aircraft, just like I've instructed hundreds of student pilots. But I wasn't depending on you for our survival. I know how to fly in pretty much any condition you could think of. I knew I wasn't going to allow us to crash."

Then he paused and continued, "With proper instruction on the outside, and a lot of self-confidence, I have no doubt, Specialist Holmes, you could learn to pilot a helicopter. But as long as you worry about crashing, you can't pilot the craft properly. So, never doubt yourself. That's the first lesson. Understood?"

"Yes. Thank you, Lieutenant."

I just flew a helicopter—damn!—I thought, as I walked with a spring in my step back to the barracks.

In my free time, in addition to playing a lot of basketball, I often hung out in the barracks with my friends, telling stories about our lives before the army, and joking about the latest happenings, and especially mishaps, on base. Occasionally we shared our hopes and dreams for the future. When we did, I imagined this was our version of what prisoners feel—serving time, waiting anxiously to be free and get on with their lives when they finally "got out." This seemed particularly true for me and my fellow draftees. We were just ordinary guys and certainly not planning on being in the army long-term. Most of us were just getting going with our adult life when Uncle Sam came calling. I felt like we were actors in an elaborate play of someone else's making.

I'd heard plenty about all the drinking and drugs in the military, especially in war zones like Vietnam. But I'd never really been into that stuff, except for some occasional drinking at college. But right now, in this army barracks, I found myself thinking that I just wanted to relax and have a little fun. It was getting late, and for some reason, the party had moved to my room. As various bottles and joints were passed around, we started playing cards and generally letting loose. A few more drinks and a few more tokes in, I watched myself accept the next thing being passed around the table and popped it into my mouth. The party continued all around me, but at an increasingly greater distance. I became aware of a surprisingly deep sense of peace filling me with joyous contentment and a heightened sense of awareness.

Ah, yes, I realized, this is what I felt when I was a kid staring up at the night sky in Neptune. Everything is connected.

As the music and clammer of the party faded into the distance, I stood up and walked outside. Looking up into the vast universe beyond our little planet, I was increasingly aware of the connections among everything around me and up in the sky. I watched each object morph into swirling patterns of energy interacting with one another, from the nearest tree to the farthest star.

It was all so beautifully captivating and energizing, I wanted to share what I was experiencing with one of my friends who had joined me outside. As I turned towards him, searching for the words to explain what was happening, he said matter-of-factly, "Oh yes, I know." And I saw in his eyes that he did. He responded this way to everything I said about my experience until he was saying "yes" even before I spoke.

"Is he teasing me or egging me on to amuse himself?" I wondered for a moment. But when I looked at him again, he became an achingly beautiful dance of energy, punctuated by a solid point of light in the immense space between his eyes. There was no logical explanation for what was happening, or how it was even possible. I became aware of a single consciousness or "being" present and operating in both our bodies at the same moment. The separation between him and me, and our separateness from "others" ceased to exist. The idea of *others* had no meaning here. There was simply a single, all-encompassing, conscious energy sitting in peaceful silence—no conflict, no differences—only the profound and overarching sense of oneness.

This consciousness expanded to include all the other people in the barracks—no matter where they were or what they were doing. I walked around base, connecting with "others," and recognizing the same consciousness in each of us. The notion of separate individual identities was embraced by a deeper, more all-encompassing experience of wholeness. A passing thought of the all-pervasive energy we studied in physics class appeared and vanished. There were no words adequate to approximate this reality.

There was only knowing this deeper inner self to be true and real. Everything else appeared to be a manifestation of that.

For a fleeting moment, my mind questioned the experience, as if it wanted to regain control. This can't be real. It's not possible, it offered weakly. The graceful and good feeling of this experience brought me gently back to a knowing awareness—one I'd forgotten, or perhaps not yet believed to be fully real. The deep contentment and achingly beautiful joy I felt was exquisitely fulfilling. A phrase from my early days in the church drifted through my mind. "The peace of God that surpasses all understanding."

Then, no more words were needed—as if even just uttering a sound would tarnish the beauty of what I knew in the core of my being to be true and life-changing. There was only this one deep, inner tranquility and unending connection to all things.

As the intensity of the experience subsided, a more normal kind of awareness returned. But nothing was quite the same, though all the familiar outward forms remained intact. What I'd witnessed had strangely altered my perspective on the very nature of reality. The familiar axioms of physics, like "energy can neither be created nor destroyed," took on new significance. And Einstein's notion of mass as another form of energy was no longer just an interesting idea; it had become a lived reality for me.

Intuitively I knew my experience was, beyond a doubt, real and would somehow serve as a pathway to answering my most pressing questions. But I couldn't fathom what I was supposed to do with this new way of seeing the world. Even as the full impact of it faded, its impression remained as a kind of "knowing" who I was at my core. I mulled over the situation and concluded: I'm still in the army. There's still a war going on in Vietnam. I have a life to sort out and live. I have a basketball game to play tomorrow. Damn, it's going to take some time to make sense out of all this.

This was clearly not the outcome I had expected going into the military. I'd figured my time in the army would be two years of living hell, and honestly, I was just hoping I would live through it. Instead, I felt like I'd reached a major turning point in my life. I had tried to "do my best and forget all the other nonsense," and oddly enough, it had made all the difference. In fact, when it came time to leave the army, along with my discharge papers, they awarded me a Certificate of Achievement for efforts "above and beyond the call of duty."

With an unapologetic grin, I cranked up the volume on my eight-track tape player and gleefully drove my newly purchased, fire-engine-red Mustang out the front gates of Fort Wolters for the last time. As Richie Havens belted out the familiar chorus of his most famous Woodstock anthem, "Freedom. Fre-e-e-e-e-d-o-o-o-o-o-m," I took a final look in my rearview mirror and happily began my fourteen-hour drive from the rolling hills of Texas to the Jersey Shore. I loved the fact that Havens had spontaneously created this iconic rendition simply because the other performers had been delayed, and in the process, set his already successful career alight.

Each moment of my homeward journey was captured in that one, beautiful word—FREEDOM! No more chain-of-command. No more officers to salute. No more protocol. Just the long road ahead and a stack of my favorite eight-track tapes in the seat beside me—the Temptations, Smokey Robinson, the Supremes, Martha and the Vandellas, the Grateful Dead, the Almond Brothers, the Band, the Moody Blues, the Beatles. It was a very large stack.

Out poured a host of feelings as I headed east—anger, confusion, joy, relief, gratitude—emotions that had been rumbling inside for two long years. My experience in the military was neither all good nor all bad, and I recalled, and perhaps understood more clearly, what Charles Dickens meant when he wrote,

> It was the best of times. It was the worst of times. It was the age of wisdom...It was the season of light, it was the season of darkness, it was the spring of hope, it was the winter of despair.

I could have engraved that quote on my wall. Life was going to be filled with challenges, for sure. But also, with opportunities to learn and grow. My time in the army had made that point clear. Knowing the military's intricate and by-the-books system of rules and regulations—inside and out—had allowed me to help other people successfully navigate their way through. I was very cool with that role. If I had to be put through a meat grinder like this, I figured, at least I could do some good. I enjoyed helping other guys—drafted and enlisted—make their way through what most often felt like a baffling labyrinth. It was a very empowering experience.

Yes, I tumbled and bumbled my way through. But at the same time, I learned a lot about myself and other people, and the actual nuts-and-bolts of how to build a highly functioning team. I gained real-life, on-the-job insights into the dynamics of organizational life, group dynamics, and human development. And I'd come to see there are many more ways to think and be than what I'd learned about prior to my time in the army. I learned I could take steps to change my life for the better, under even the most difficult circumstances. I also realized that finding and following a positive purpose for my life with confidence and skills is what would make all the difference for me.

In addition, my inner spiritual awakening introduced me to what felt like a long-forgotten inner reality connecting me to others. This growing way of seeing and living in the world was the cornerstone I wanted to build my life upon, like the wise man in Jesus's parable, who "built his house on the solid rock." Funny that these teachings heard so long ago in Sunday school were now making so much sense to me. But what do I do with all this? Where, exactly, do you go, to learn how to lean into this way of being and living in the world?

6

DEFYING GRAVITY

I could go along, to avoid a confrontation. But why fall back into old patterns of behavior? Nope. It was time to make a choice—come what may.

I made my way home, and my family was pleased and relieved to have me back. I sat with them, bathing in their company—happy just to be with them again. Surviving the army without being shot at and without firing a weapon—except in training—was more than I had hoped for. And now I felt safe. I could relax—play a little pickup basketball, chill, read books, listen to music, catch up with friends—with no one barking orders and telling me what to do.

Early the next morning in the kitchen, Mom gave me fair warning.

"You know," she said, looking over the rim of her glasses with kindness and empathy, "your dad wants to paint the house. He'll want you to help."

KA-BOOM!

Ah yes, Dad has plans…and they include me. I felt some air go out of my tires.

He found me soon enough.

"Son, it's good to have you back home. I was thinking, the house really could do with a painting. Now that you're home, we can do it together. No hurry. Take a couple of days to settle in, and then we can get started. Your brother Ralph will help too."

Deja vu all over again, I thought.

Dad was happy for everything to go back to normal, meaning I would fit in like the old days. And since I was neither in the army nor away at college, I could do jobs around the house as he saw fit. To a certain degree, that was fine, but I'd just spent the last two years of my life following orders in total service to the army. I felt tired to the bone and was not in the mood for some new—or old—chain of command, parents or otherwise.

While I was away, my dad and my younger brother, Ralph, spent lots of time together working on Dad's boat and various other projects. Ralph genuinely loved it, and I was happy for them both. But that was them being who they are, and this...well, this was me, still looking for who I was. The thought of climbing up and down a ladder with a paint bucket and brush for the next few weeks was more than I could bear. I just couldn't do it. Not now. I needed time—and space—to just be me, whoever that was at this point in my life.

I *could* go along, to avoid a confrontation. But why fall back into old patterns of behavior? Nope. It was time to make a choice—come what may.

And that's precisely when Reggie, my best friend from the FDU basketball team, called from out of the blue.

"Hey, Whole-Man. What are you up to?"

"Reggie? Dude. I just got out of the army. Where are you?"

"California, man. Why don't you come out here? I got sun. I got a great pad. I got all kinds of fun. There are plenty of beautiful women just waiting to meet you. Everything is beautiful, man. Why don't you come to California?"

"Hmm, sounds cool," I said. "Let me think about it, Reg. I'll get back to you."

I knew the answer to Reggie's question before we hung up. This was just what the doctor ordered. I had always really wanted to see California. And besides, it would get me out of having to paint the house with Ralph and my dad, which I knew would feel like *extra duty*, as if I was back in the army. Go West, young man. Go West!

Heading off to college had been the first big step out of my comfort zone of home, and I was excited to go for it. Then the army came storming along—taking me on a wild and unforeseen adventure. And now this new chapter was beginning—whatever *this* was. But the pull of family, friends, and the familiar was strong, and I knew from the laws of physics that the first and biggest challenge to successful space travel is breaking free of the Earth's gravitational forces. "Well, here I am, sitting on the launch pad, ready and waiting to explore the unknown," I thought. "So, what's holding me back?" For one thing, flying coast-to-coast was way too expensive. And buses and trains are painfully slow. I needed something fast *and* cheap.

Then it came to me. What about driving my faithful Mustang? Gas is cheap. Dirt cheap. And I can plan my own route, see the sights along the way, and have the adventure of a lifetime. All those amazing places I've heard and read about—the Rockies, the Grand Canyon, the Painted Desert. Plus, maybe I'll find what I'm looking for out west with my old friend Reggie?

I bought a map and penciled in my route. Where this trip might lead, I wasn't sure. But I had to start somewhere and work out the details as they unfolded. The scientists and astronauts at NASA, I'm sure, were more detailed in their planning. But my destination was more modest, and I was committed to taking off in search of new opportunities.

I wondered though—with my two years of military service and Reggie's additional two years of partying—how would we actually get on with one another? One thing was a given—we were bound to have some fun. It was always fun around Reggie. And isn't that just what I need right about now…some fun? Hanging out in sunny Southern California sounds pretty great—maybe even therapeutic? Besides, I sincerely wanted to see America's vastness.

Over the next couple of days, I got the Mustang ready—filled it with gas, changed the oil, checked the water and hoses, bought spare parts. The drive from New Jersey to California was over three thousand miles. But with gas at twenty-five cents per gallon, and my Mustang getting twenty-five miles to the gallon, the whole trip—there *and* back—would cost me less than a hundred bucks.

Satisfied with my preparations, I was ready to take care of one final little detail—to tell my dad. I found him hard at work out in the backyard.

"Dad, my friend Reggie has invited me to spend some time with him in California this summer before I go back to college."

Dad knew Reggie. Reggie had lived with us and worked with me in the Bell Labs kitchen where my dad was chef. Dad trusted Reggie, so that was a point in my favor.

"I told him yes. I'm leaving tomorrow morning."

Confusion and disappointment quickly clouded my dad's face, and I felt a twinge of guilt pass over me.

"California? That's a long way away, son. How're you going to get out there? Are you going alone? It doesn't make a lot of sense to me. That's going to cost you a lot of money, son."

Here we go again, I thought. He doesn't think I know what I'm doing. And he doesn't seem to get why I'm doing it. At least that's how it feels. A wave of contradictory thoughts flooded my mind. Maybe he's right. Maybe I don't know what I'm doing. Is this whole space launch thing a dumb—maybe even dangerous—idea?

Standing there in the shadow of our lovely, little white house with black shutters—the home I'd known and loved since I was fourteen—I felt the gravity of home drawing me away from what I wanted—and felt I needed—to do, to launch the next phase of my life. Yes, there were risks, but was that a good enough reason to stay?

I looked around at the immaculately kept green grass my dad so proudly labored over and gathered my courage to explain myself.

"Dad, I'd like to help paint the house, but I really need a break right now. I worked hard in the military for the past two years and I've been under a lot of stress. I need some time to myself."

I hoped I'd made my point clear.

"I understand, son," he responded, without skipping a beat, "but driving all the way to California and back? That's not going to be much of a break, is it? I think you'd be better off staying here getting some rest and home-cooked food and helping me and your brother Ralph paint the house."

I felt a sharp twinge of hurt and anger rising up in me and then, surprisingly, a small sliver of insight, along with all those other familiar feelings. Dad's logic is actually pretty sound, I mused. At least if we're only considering his point of view to be valid. So, it's not that he's wrong...or right, or that he's trying to be mean. He's just not accepting my point of view and my opinions as being valid, and isn't that what really hurts? Wow, how did I not see this for all these years? In the past, his outer judgements and my inner doubts would have stopped me in my tracks. But somehow, this time around, I could see it was just Dad expressing his own opinion. A well-intentioned offering that I could accept or not—my choice. It was difficult, but I knew what I had to do.

"Thanks, Dad," I said, trying to sound as nonchalant as possible. "I appreciate your point of view, but I've got the Mustang ready to go. I'm driving. I'm all set."

"Well, if that's what you want to do, son." His look was one of deep disappointment. But I'd faced him man to man and stood my ground, and I felt a heavy weight lifted from my shoulders and a deep surge of agency rising in my heart.

Bright and early the following morning, I hopped into the Mustang and headed for the New Jersey Turnpike. I was excited and felt a kind of lightness I hadn't experienced in a long while. The northern route, Interstate 80, was fastest, and felt safest. No telling what the older southern highways and roads would throw my way. Bumping into the mentality of "Whites Only" signs, literally or figuratively, was not what I wanted to confront. Not on this trip, thank you very much.

Averaging fourteen hours a day, with my eight-track player churning out the tunes, I figured I could steer my way steadily across the countryside, take in the sights, and be in California by dinner time on day four.

The days were long, but the drive west felt easy, even relaxing. My eyes were wide open. And I felt my heart opening to the expansiveness of the land that was my birthright. This was my country, my heritage, and I wanted to see it in its fullness.

Crossing the Mississippi River, I stood amazed under the Gateway Arch in St. Louis, marking the halfway point across the continent. My long drive through the endless cornfields of Iowa and Nebraska went on, and on, and on. One giant, flat, yellow-and-green tapestry spreading out to the horizon in every direction.

But I knew where I was headed next, and my fear of heights warned of a sudden change in elevation as I edged nearer the Rocky Mountains. The great range came into view some fifty miles short of Denver—the "Mile High City."

Man, oh man, I thought, if they're this huge from way out here, where it's this flat, what will they be like up close? And how will I ever get over them?

A vicious hailstorm hurled down marbles of ice pounding out across the plains. The cattle ran for cover in their feedlots, but there was none to be found. I pulled the Mustang to the side of the road and under a thin, thirsty tree. As the storm let up and finally passed, I saw another enormous pile of clouds looming up in front of me.

Oh, I realized with some alarm, as I continued to stare down the highway, those are the Rockies—covered in snow —not clouds at all. They're even more majestic than I'd imagined.

I skirted Denver and continued the westward climb, feeling the pounding heartbeat of my skyward journey. What surprises were waiting for me? What perils? In a moment of daring, I turned off the interstate in favor of the local roads.

To get a better feel for what being in the Rockies is all about, I mused.

What they're about, I soon discovered, was giant rocks jutting sharply out into a surprisingly narrow and ever-curving roadway on one side. And an endless number of perilously steep cliffs dropping thousands of feet along the other side—with no guard rails to provide some semblance of safety.

Out—sharply in—then instantly out again—the slender slip of road wound its way haplessly upwards—at ever-steeper gradients. The atmosphere grew breathless and thin, and like me, my little Mustang began gasping for ample oxygen to make the strenuous climb. Pedal to the metal—we were barely making thirty miles an hour.

Should I get out and push? How would that even work?

And what was so wrong with the interstate, anyway?

So winding was the dainty mountain pass and so intense my concentration around each hair-pin turn, the beauty and grandeur of the Rockies was lost on me that day. Around dusk, I found a place to stop and set up camp for the night. As I climbed out to stretch my stiff limbs, I discovered my hands in a death grip around the steering wheel.

Relax, I chanted. Just relax.

I slept like a rock and got on the road early. By noon, my frazzled mind and tired body were growing more accustomed to the rigors of mountain driving. I began leaning into the curves, judging my speed and distance more accurately, and steering with less anxiety. I began experimenting—steering one-handed on the short straightaways while flexing and resting the other hand.

The Mustang continued climbing sluggishly, but even she seemed a bit more at ease. As my "flat-lander" survival instincts decreased, my appreciation and enjoyment of the extraordinary landscape surrounding me steadily expanded. By sunset, I was back on a more even footing, at a lower altitude, and headed south-southwest toward the "Four Corners," the place where four states—Colorado, New Mexico, Arizona, and Utah—meet at their corners.

Meandering down through Navajo and Hopi territory the following day, I marveled at the regal geologic outcroppings and mesas formed along ancient seashores. Farther south, the Painted Desert jumped to life, as band over band of every imaginable color—purple, lavender, gray, brown, red, orange, pink—shimmered in a grand parade of earthen rainbows through the hot desert air. The beauty of the scene conjured a pure sense of wonder, gratitude, and reverence.

Around lunchtime I stopped for gas and food, and called home to check in.

"Ah," my younger brother, Ralph, said with a chuckle, when he answered the phone. "So, the prodigal son honors us with a call. One minute I hear Dad say we're going to paint the house. So, I'm thinking, okay, we can knock it out pretty fast with Larry helping. I get up the next morning and—no Larry. Where did Larry go? 'Oh, he's gone to California, dear,' Mom says, with that sweet little smile of hers. Dad looks up from his paper and just shakes his head. 'That don't make no kind of sense.'"

I turned north-northeast toward the Grand Canyon and arrived well after sundown. Little could be seen, but I sensed the vastness, like an infinite vacuum in space. Exhausted, I slept in the Mustang and walked eagerly to the edge of the canyon when I woke up. My stomach dropped as my eyes struggled to take in the depth and breadth of the magnificent expanse above, before, and a full mile below me.

"How in the world is this even possible?" I marveled to myself. Like the heavens and the earth—all meeting in one awe-inspiring dance.

After breakfast, I continued north to take in the Bonneville Salt Flats—famously large and flat enough to host the regular setting of land speed records. Then I headed south again to view the glitzy casino lights of Las Vegas before barreling due west, directly into North America's driest desert—the vast Mojave Desert of Southern California. And just north of there is Death Valley, which holds the record for the highest recorded air temperature on the planet (134.1 degrees F). The challenge of this part of my journey was quite real.

Seeing other creatures or cars along the endless miles of desolate desert highway became an increasing rarity. The parched landscape was exhilarating but deeply lonely. With no air conditioning and all the windows rolled down, blasts of scorching air filled the Mustang as she hummed along. A broad body of water appeared, hovering cool and blue on the horizon—a mirage's false offering of relief from the relentless heat. Dark banks of menacing clouds rose up quickly in the distance as a stiff wind began shoving the car from side to side like a child's toy. I was confused. It looked like a giant rainstorm was headed my way...in the middle of the desert?

Before I could make sense of the situation, a swirling cloud of dust swallowed the Mustang whole and rendered the roadway invisible. Within the eerie earthen cloud, a barrage of immense raindrops began pelting the hood and windshield and mixing with the choking mass.

"It's raining mud!" I gasped aloud. "What the hell am I supposed to do now?"

In an effort to quell my rising sense of panic, I rolled my window up, lifted my foot off the accelerator, and eased the Mustang toward what I hoped was the shoulder. As I leaned across to roll up the passenger-side window, the car began rocking and shuttering violently. Moaning and groaning, the angry maelstrom threatened to hurl me and my sleek little car into oblivion. Enveloped in the twirling wall of mud, I surrendered—lashing my arms through the steering wheel, closing my eyes, holding my breath, and waiting with dread for the storm's fury to relent.

As suddenly as it started, the howling wind calmed, and I began breathing more easily. Shaken, I opened the door and climbed out to assess the damage. The wire wheels were buried in deep drifts of dust. And though caked in thick layers of red mud, the Mustang was otherwise intact. I popped the hood, replaced the air filter from my stash of spare parts, scraped off the windows and mirrors as best I could, climbed in, and started her up. New Jersey snowstorms had taught me the drill—shift into low, ease out the clutch, slow and steady wins the race—and voila, I was back on the road.

Feeling rattled and clearly at the mercy of the ever-changing elements, my mind drifted toward anxious thoughts—second-guessing the wisdom of this solo voyage into the unknown.

Ah yes, I thought, the familiar voice of fear. But this trip feels precisely like what I'm meant to be doing. I need this— to face these challenges—to find greater strength and clarity in myself. I'm on the right track. I just need to keep going.

Blowing out the dust, I popped a tape into the eight-track player, turned up the volume, and continued my trek westward. A lifting stream of enthusiasm returned to my heart. And a smile to my face.

"Hey, Whole-Man, you made it. Great to see you. Come on in, man. Make yourself at home!"

Same old Reggie. With a giant grin on his face and a very long arm around my shoulder, he welcomed me into his beautiful Orange County apartment.

"It's great to see you too, Reggie. Whoa, this place is amazing," I said, looking around and then out toward the inviting party pool just beyond his balcony.

Yep. We were going to have a good time this summer—no doubt about it.

Sitting at the fancy bar in his living room, he mixed us some drinks, and we picked up right where we'd left off two years earlier and jumped into catching up with one another.

"You look good, Whole-Man. All slim and fit. Looks like the army's been treating you okay. I've seen guys come out looking like death warmed over. That war in 'Nam—that's no joke, man."

I couldn't argue with him on that point. On the other hand, the way the army treated me was more of a mixed bag.

"So, dude, I got a great job out here," Reggie proclaimed, launching our conversation in a new direction. "I'm working for an insurance company doing sales work—nine to five. So, I've got all my nights and weekends free. Plenty of time to party. And the women out here are amazing. You're gonna love it, man."

Reggie was no longer a college student or the star of our college basketball team, but he was clearly continuing to live the lifestyle he'd been famous for at school—partying as much and as often as possible. At six-foot, six-inches tall and with a deep, booming voice, Reggie was hard to miss or ignore, and he relished being the life of any party he attended. I figured that was cool. Plus, everything I'd heard about Southern California appeared to be true—constant sunshine, fantastic beaches, and lots of beautiful people, especially the women. So, we partied. We partied hard. And often.

"What's up, Whole-man?" he bellowed from the front door when he arrived home from work. "Where're we gonna party tonight, dude? I am ready to have some fun!"

As much as I enjoyed the whole party scene, something was nagging at me. I tried getting back into it with Reggie and his friends and losing myself in the exciting times we were having. But something important was missing. Somehow, I'd moved on. My challenging circumstances and profound spiritual experience in the army had changed me, and I found myself at fancy gatherings filled with happy people, silently wondering, what am I doing here? And why?

I'd covered more ground in the past two years than I realized. Reggie saw the same old Whole-man on the outside. But inside, I simply wasn't the same person. Reggie seemed to find himself early in life and stuck with it. Would he ever get serious? Why should he? His whole purpose and intention was simply to enjoy life and have a good time. He was just being who he'd always been—good old, fun-loving Reggie. *That* Reggie was great for me in college. But the questions that filled my head and heart were no longer about which party to go to, what hip people might be attending, or how many beautiful females would be there. I knew those bases would all be covered. Reggie would make sure of that!

Instead, I found myself contemplating the deeper meaning of my life. Who am I? Where am I going? What is my purpose? Being drafted had taught me that life could take sudden and unexpected turns. Especially if I wasn't fully awake and actively steering. Intuitively I knew this lifestyle, though fun, was not what I wanted, or needed.

By late summer, I said my goodbyes to Reggie and drove north to San Francisco to make one last important stop before heading east. Haight Ashbury was considered the center of the counterculture movement in America, and I wanted to experience it up close and personal. As I walked around the district, I met people of various ages, races, colors, genders, and persuasions—interacting in ways different than I was used to seeing. Most appeared to be just hanging out. Many were wearing hippie attire, smoking joints, playing music, and clearly enjoying the colorful scene. What struck me most, was their lack of criticism or judgment toward one another. Instead, I sensed a kind of acceptance, a sense of community and togetherness that felt good and right. Everyone I approached responded with warmth and openness.

"How's it going? Hey, where are you from, man? What's your name? You want to hang out with us?" This attitude felt closer to what I sensed was needed in the world. But I wondered too, how this laid-back approach would help address the pressing issues of our times? Where's the plan? I wondered. What actions could be taken to address the countless social, economic, and political challenges in some positive, tangible way? Something felt like it was missing.

The return trip from Southern California to the Jersey Shore was a straight shot and included little sightseeing and lots of long hours of driving. As my trusty Mustang and I hummed down the highway, I contemplated some thread I was following in my mind. It had something to do with freedom and wholeness, but the way forward was elusive, like walking across a bridge but building it at the same time. Where would I be when I got to the other side?

I found myself longing to find a career path in harmony with who I was becoming and all that I'd experienced and learned the past two years. I was eager to get home, relaunch my college studies, and chart a course for the next phase of my life. The desire to find a deeper sense of purpose for my life drove me forward. There was work to be done, and I was ready to roll up my sleeves and get on with it.

7

FORKS IN THE ROAD

"You don't need to label yourself a radical, revolutionary, or anything else for that matter. It's not the label that makes a difference. Keep speaking and living the truth based on your own life experience. That will have the most impact."

My initial research into schools and programs of study led me to something called developmental and social psychology. I dug a bit deeper and concluded the University of Michigan in Ann Arbor would be the ideal place for me. It had a world-class psychology program, and a newly-conceived, innovative, and highly-regarded liberal arts program called the Residential College. The classes there were typically interdisciplinary. Plus, Michigan had a reputation for being one of the most radical campuses in the country—a hotbed of political, social, and counter-cultural activity—all newly awakened interests of mine. Senator John F. Kennedy, I discovered, had proposed a bold new branch of public service called the Peace Corps while visiting Ann Arbor during his bid to become president. It seems to be a place where things happen. Damn, I thought, this sounds perfect.

But a big hurdle stood in my way. My tussle with physics and especially mathematics at FDU had pulled my grade-point average down considerably. If I wanted to get into Michigan, I needed to get my grades back up—and fast. My best option, I figured, was to go to a smaller school for a year or so, study hard, get good grades, and then transfer to Michigan.

I'd always admired the picturesque beauty of New England and its centuries-old academic tradition, and I started researching colleges in the area that might be appropriate. One in particular seemed to be a good fit, so I applied and was accepted into Western New England College in Springfield, Massachusetts. The fact that the NBA Hall of Fame happens to be located in Springfield felt like an added bonus. Touring the place and feeling the weight of all the photos and paraphernalia of great stars of the past was a great experience.

Another hurdle was money. Thanks to my stint in the army, the GI Bill would cover a significant part of my school expenses. To make up the difference, though, a good paying job was on my list of things I needed to figure out. I was keen on paying my own way, going forward. That, I was sure, was best for both me and my folks.

During my last two years of high school, I had a great summer job connecting and disconnecting phone lines in an indoor Bell Telephone facility. It was good money, and I'd felt good about working there and being accepted by the older, long-term workers. I checked into it and was told they were only hiring for external installers. That would be a lot more technically and physically demanding than my high school job, but it also paid better.

They started me off with four weeks of training to make sure I was able to climb up and down utility poles, run wires, and connect into their network safely.

"Stepped" poles, I discovered, are a piece of cake, because they have metal spikes driven into alternate sides, allowing you to climb up to the junction box with ease.

On the other hand, "unstepped" poles—mostly in the older neighborhoods—require special climbing gear strapped around each leg, with sharp metal gaffs that dig into the wood and allow you to climb your way up the pole.

One thing my instructors underscored more than once was that if you don't insert the gaffs at precisely the right angle, they don't go in deep enough to hold your weight, and you can slide uncontrollably back down the pole. This little fact added to my fear of heights and general feelings of uneasiness about the job. Most poles were twenty-five or thirty feet off the ground. Still, my safety harness was of some comfort, and it also helped to know I was physically fit. It'll be fine, I told myself.

Training ended, and I was issued my own truck, outfitted with all the tools needed for most installation or repair jobs. It was springtime on the Jersey Shore. I was well paid and on my own, and I was feeling quite giddy about the whole situation. A few weeks into the new work routine, I was at the top of a tall, unstepped pole on a bright sunny morning, preparing to connect a wire to the home of a new customer. Further down the line a raucous crow scolded me from the top of another pole. An omen? I leaned back in my safety harness and reached overhead with both arms to make the junction box connection. My gaffs gave way, and for one long, terrifying moment, I was free falling.

A few feet below my harness caught and slammed me into the pole as my flailing arms and legs fought to find a hold. Catching my breath, I hugged the pole tightly and made a desperate attempt to kick one of my gaffs in. It ricocheted off, and I bumped quickly down the pole a few more feet.

"Damn, damn, damn!" I yelled and wrapped my arms more tightly around the pole. There I hung, dangling, and holding on for dear life.

They warned us in training that this "close-up, vertical angle to the pole" is the most unstable and difficult to recover from. I fully believed them and began to wonder how long I could last before sliding the remaining distance to the ground below.

I pondered the headline in tomorrow's paper: "Local Boy Returns Home from Army Safely Only to Fall to His Death from Telephone Pole."

I tried again to get one of my gaffs to bite. And then again, and again, and again.

And then, as my screaming arms and shoulders and back began to falter, I got one to stick. With a rush of relief, I gathered my strength, got my second gaff to grab, and made my way slowly down.

Once again on solid ground, I packed my gear, climbed into my truck, drove to the depot, and—without looking at my next service order—turned in my resignation, and drove my trusty Mustang back home. It felt like the only right thing to do.

"Hi, honey. Did you get off early?" asked Mom as I slipped in the kitchen through the side door.

"Yeah, I did, Mom."

Technically, it was true. The whole incident felt too raw to get into it with her. I turned around and left the same way I came.

While I was out, my dad came home. My supervisor stopped by too. Dad talked to him. My supervisor told him I'd suddenly resigned, and he couldn't understand it.

"He's a good worker—a good technician, and he's good with all the tools too. I can't figure out what happened. Why would he just up and quit like that?"

Dad met me at the door when I got home a few hours later.

"Your supervisor drove over. He was wondering why you resigned. He said you were doing good. What happened, son?"

I told him about my battle with the pole and figured he'd see my point of view once he heard about the physical danger I'd just faced.

"But you've got a good job, son," my dad offered. "And you're obviously respected by your boss. He made a special trip out here just to talk to you. Plus, you're making good money."

I was at a loss for words. What more could I say to him?

"You need that job to pay for college, don't you? What will you do now, son?"

A very good question. What came to mind was our family trips to Florida to see our grandmother and great-grandmother, and the feelings of shock and sadness their poverty provoked in me. It began to sink in. That was the world Mom and Dad grew up in. And my siblings and I enjoyed a very different life experience, thanks to their tireless efforts. Our parents' lives are based on the struggle to survive, I surmised. Creating a close-knit, safe, and successful family is their number one goal. And becoming a successful and upstanding person in the community, admired by others—is a close second. These are the things that would have felt impossible to achieve for a black person when they were growing up, and they happily did whatever was necessary to change the situation for us kids. They provided a secure foundation and wanted us to have access to all the material things that they never had as children.

It was a painful realization, but I began to grasp my dad's point of view at a deeper level, though it was still annoying, and at times like this, felt stifling. Up on that telephone pole, with my life hanging in the balance, survival was my top goal too. But Mom and Dad grew up with some version of that challenge, real or perceived, every day. By providing me with the opportunities, possibilities, and relative safety not available to them, my perspectives, expectations, and values were different. Not necessarily right or wrong—just different.

"I don't know, Dad," I said quietly. "I'll just find something else to do."

Truthfully, I had no idea what I'd find. All I knew for certain was that life was trying to teach me something important. What was it? I was learning that change has to start somewhere, with someone, at some point in time. And it's very seldom easy. I was struggling to find the courage to break free of the old pattern—doing as I've been told and not rocking the boat—with my dad especially. This experience was definitely shaking me out of my comfort zone. I could no longer stay with the known, especially if the known included pole climbing. Such a traumatic event was making it clear. It was time to move on. Time to do what felt right for me.

If not here, where? If not now, when? It was time to seize the day.

My head and heart needed clearing, and for me that meant one thing—playing some hoops. I hopped in the Mustang and headed to the nearby outdoor courts where some of the better players—including college guys and even a few pros—gathered for pickup games most evenings.

"Hey, Larry, you ready to run, man?" Ha, I thought, you have *no* idea.

With a grin on his face, Ron Kornagay greeted me in this way most evenings we played together. He stood at five-seven, but Ron was devastatingly quick, and a very talented ball handler and shooter. And he was a nice guy. He was also ever eager to "school" others on their defensive skills whenever he got the chance. We often played with my high school mentor, Henry Moore. Each game felt like a chess match, testing my physical skills, and probing my heart and mind as a player. It was exhilarating, and exhausting, and hands down my most favorite time of the day. It was just the kind of therapy I was looking for.

Ron proceeded to "school me good," as he said, and one day, afterward, one of my favorite high school teachers walked by. We'd known each other since I was in sixth grade, and he'd been one of my most helpful high school coaches too.

"Hey, Larry, it's great to see you again. What're you up to these days?"

"Well, I was drafted—I guess you heard? I just got out of two years in the army. So, now I'm looking for work and hoping to go back to college next fall. I'm looking at Western New England College."

"That's great, man. I'm glad to see you getting your education back on track. And if you need some money, I've got just the thing. You wanna do some substitute teaching in the Neptune and Asbury Park school system?"

I laughed out loud.

"I did *not* see that coming, Coach. I'm definitely not a teacher."

"What? You'd be great at it. And we can really use your help, Larry. We're really short on substitutes this spring. You've got a couple of years of college under your belt, right? That's not even a possibility for most of these kids. It's just a one-page application, and I'd be happy to get the ball rolling for you. I'll put in a good word too. Whaddya say? Give it a go?"

He was clearly seeing something in me that I wasn't feeling in myself. All I could picture was how much I'd struggled as a physics major at FDU. On the other hand, what did I have to lose? I really needed the cash. Plus, no more climbing or dangling from poles.

"Okay, Coach, thanks. Why not? I'll give it a try."

"Sweet. I'll get things going for you."

My first call came at 7:00 a.m. a week later.

"Good morning, Mr. Holmes, this is the principal's office at Neptune High. We've got a teacher who's called in sick this morning. Are you available to substitute?"

"Yes ma'am, I'm on my way," I said, holding back a yawn.

Okay, here we go. I showered, dressed, selected one of my few ties, and headed to my alma mater up the street.

Standing in front of a class of young high schoolers for the first time felt weird. I found myself thinking about the teachers I'd had in this same building. The ones who'd really understood and encouraged me. And others, like my history teacher, who couldn't seem to see past the color of my skin and the biases that often come with it. As I called roll and focused on each young face, their potential, it seemed, was all I could see. For many of them, something else was there too, standing in their path, like a shadow—a very low view of themselves—often covered over by loud and abrasive bravado, and I knew in my heart, it was not totally of their own making.

Ah yes, I thought, I've been here, right where you are. And now I'm back, but not just to keep order in the classroom, which is definitely needed. This is more. I was looking for the goodness in them, even if they didn't see it themselves...to help them recognize the possibilities in themselves. I wanted to share or awaken the same kind of light that Henry and many others shared with me.

I was kept busy as a substitute teacher for the rest of the school year. And my high school gig led me to a summer job at Brookdale Community College teaching—of all things—mathematics—the nemesis of my short run at FDU. So, now I'm teaching it? The irony was not lost on me.

It was odd, but what surprised me most—I liked it. I found that I was actually pretty good at it. Slowly the notion of being a teacher began to feel like something I might want to pursue. Teaching, I began to believe, is about helping people understand—and imbibe—what's being taught, not just putting a bunch of information out there and hoping something sticks. I dedicated myself to making sure my students truly understood the material we were covering. This is what was mostly missing in my education, I thought.

And as I began to step away from limiting ideas about myself, I saw it was helping my students do the same. Whoa, I'm doing it, I thought. I might actually be getting the hang of, and perhaps the deeper purpose behind this teaching thing.

By Labor Day of 1972, my boxes and bags were packed. The summer math classes I was teaching at Brookdale Community College had ended, and as the summer wound its way down, I said my goodbyes to family and friends and headed to Western New England College. The Mustang and I happily made our way north, as bright autumn colors began appearing around each bend—reds, oranges, and golden yellows. The rich smell of burning leaves hung sweetly in the crisp, autumn air.

"When you come to a fork in the road…" I mused with a grin, "…take it!" Pondering this humorous bit of wisdom from the famous baseball star Yogi Berra, I realized this was definitely my fork in the road. I felt excited and nervous all at the same time. Excited to be pursuing a course of study of my own choosing. Nervous because I wondered if I was headed in the right direction. Was psychology really "it" for me? And could I actually succeed at college this time around? I had doubts, yes. On the other hand, I felt up for the challenge and oddly ready to begin another journey into the unknown. I was taking the fork.

Driving through Western New England's campus for the first time, I was bedazzled. Beautiful, old, brick buildings stood in dignified groupings and provided a weighty sense of permanence and belonging to the carefully manicured lawns and hedges. Mazes of wide brick walkways crisscrossed through the landscape, connecting elegant granite steps, solemnly arched gates and porticos, and heavy oak doorways. Ancient, muscular trees stood watch in all directions, their magnificent fall colors ablaze in the warm, afternoon sunlight. The scale and grandeur of the place and small number of students—just twenty-five hundred—created an elegant air of luxurious spaciousness.

Not too shabby. Not too shabby at all, I thought. Looks like I landed on my feet.

I registered, got my room assignment and key, unpacked the Mustang, and settled in. My roommate was welcoming and pleasant, and it felt good to be back in school again—come what may.

Most of my fellow students gave me a wide berth the first few weeks of class. There was nothing that felt intentionally mean or rude in it. As one of just a handful of African American students on campus, I was clearly "different." Not being there on an athletic scholarship was also an oddity. I was several years older than most of my classmates too, and my former army haircut had blossomed into a rather sizable Afro in keeping with the groovy times. I often wore parts of my old army fatigues along with a pair of dark sunglasses and a stern gaze in keeping with the Black Power zeitgeist of the late 1960s and early 1970s. To my fellow students, I have to imagine, I looked a bit prickly.

I found myself once again gravitating toward the table of mostly African American students in the cafeteria, out of habit, I guess. I introduced myself and sat down.

"Hey man, where ya' from? What's your major? We saw you on the basketball court the other day—you've got some nice moves. Are you here to play ball? What's your story, man?" I became aware that basketball was becoming like a calling card that a large segment of people could relate to and feel comfortable with. It often seemed to break the ice with people despite my more reserved personality.

I kept my story short, but we talked for quite a while, and the familiar banter commenced before long. It felt good to be hanging out together. It also felt like I was stuck in a time warp. Why, I wondered, am I sitting at the "Black Table?" Habit? Comfort? Am I really that same guy I was in high school? I don't think so. Hasn't my life experience been a little broader and deeper?

Over time, I got to know a lot of the kids on my dorm floor and in some of my classes too. I began to make a point to introduce myself to people I didn't know, and slowly, other students started introducing themselves to me. Yes, I was different. But I was clearly making an effort to be open and nonjudgemental, and that seemed to make them curious.

Word got out that I'd been in the military before coming to Western New England College. It was the early 1970s, and the antiwar movement was spreading like wildfire on college campuses across the country. Western New England was no exception. Several students approached me in the cafeteria one afternoon looking for some answers.

"So, Larry, we heard you were drafted. That's crazy. What was it like? Did you have to fight? What do you think about the war in Vietnam?"

Whoa. That's a lot of questions.

"Yes," I began. "I was drafted and served two years in the army. I was lucky though. I didn't have to fight. But I'm close friends with guys that did. War is terrible, but I'm not into looking down on people for serving their country."

They just stood there looking at me.

"Any more questions?" I added.

"Yes. Can you speak at our next antiwar rally on campus? You're the real deal, Larry. You've actually served in the army during the Vietnam conflict. People should hear what you've got to say."

I didn't see that coming.

The following week, I found myself standing behind a microphone on the steps of the Student Union Building in front of hundreds of students and faculty.

"Good afternoon," I began, a little too quietly.

I looked up. People were cupping their hands behind their ears, straining to hear.

"I was drafted into the army..." I said, leaning into the mic.

My voice boomed out over the campus grounds, and people covered their ears as the speakers on stage let loose a torrent of high-pitched feedback. I stopped, stood up straight, and started over.

"Good afternoon. My name is Larry Holmes, and I was drafted into the army. I served our country for two years. I'm here today because I think it's important to highlight the difference between being against the war but not being against the guys who are fighting in it, or against our country."

People lowered their hands. Some cocked their heads.

"My experience is that being a member of the military does not necessarily mean you're a war monger or a bad person. Most of the soldiers serving in the military have volunteered to be there to serve their country and are doing the best job they know how under some very difficult circumstances. They are engaging in jungle warfare with people who were born and live and were trained as soldiers in their own country.

"It's true that a certain percentage of draftees are from minorities and lower income backgrounds. So, there is a certain shock and horror when you're in one or both of those groups, and it happens to you. I am one of those draftees. However, I was fortunate enough to not have to actually go fight in Vietnam under those dangerous circumstances. But what's the point of criticizing fellow citizens serving their country—either those who genuinely volunteered to serve, or those who've been drafted into service through no choice of their own? Either way, a soldier may be faced with the awful choice of killing or being killed in a battle situation. Who here would say that such a choice would sit easily with them? The real question is who has the power to put them in that situation, and why would they choose to do so?"

I let the question hang for a moment. "My experience during my time in the army has led me to believe that it's our government's policies and strategies that are failing the American people—and the people of Vietnam too—not the soldiers themselves. Soldiers are merely the blunt human instruments used to carry out these ill-conceived policies. Thank you for listening."

I sat down and looked around. My speech seemed to resonate with my fellow students. Lots of them were standing up and clapping, and some were holding a fist in the air as a sign of solidarity. I'd never been into public speaking or politics before, especially radical politics. But I heard my own words and the passion in my voice, and I began to see another side of myself. The editor of the school newspaper approached me when the rally ended.

"Hey, Larry, I'm with *The Westerner*, the student paper here at the college. I really like what you said. And the way you said it. Would you like to write a column for the paper? We'd love to hear your thoughts on a regular basis."

I was very surprised. I didn't see that coming.

"Well," I said, "writing isn't really my thing, but I'll think about it. Thanks."

Inside I thought, I'm definitely not a writer. Sure, I've got plenty of thoughts floating around in my head. But putting them down on paper? I don't know about that.

After the next rally, the editor asked me again to write a column, and I found myself saying, "Okay, I'll give it a go."

What's the worst that can happen? I wondered. They could fire me, I suppose. But then I'd just be back where I started, and no worse for the wear. Who knows, I might even learn something in the process?

It wasn't easy, but as a result of these opportunities, I began speaking more openly about what I was seeing and experiencing in my own life. As a result, it became clearer that these were the challenges that caused so many of us, black and white, men and women, young and old, to suffer. I used my speech notes as the outlines for my newspaper editorials. I was letting go of a few more limiting notions of myself and daring to be vulnerable through my public writing and speaking in hopes of encouraging others to do the same. How else can we start to make a difference?

It seems no matter how far from home you go, news about what you're up to finds its way back. In a hurry. When I returned to Neptune for the fall break, my dad approached me with great concern on his face and in his voice.

"What you doin' up at that college, son?"

Uh oh, I thought.

"What do you mean, Dad?"

"Bob called me over to his office to speak with him today. It was all about you."

Hmm, this can't be good. Bob was a close, long-time friend of my dad's. He was also African American and a captain on the local police force.

"Bob says a couple of guys from the FBI were asking a bunch of questions down at the police station. Questions about you, Larry. Questions about rallies and demonstrations that you've supposedly been involved in up at that college."

His voice was tight. It was evident that he was very concerned. I definitely did not want to get into a political argument with my dad.

"They investigate everybody that does anything, Dad," I suggested. "Some students asked me to talk about my time in the army. So I did." I played it down.

"You better be careful, son. That's all."

He was right. J. Edgar Hoover was director of the FBI at the time, and anyone who showed even the slightest of political leanings unsupportive of current government policies was under suspicion of being a dangerous radical and potentially a communist.

So, now *this* is happening? *This* is happening to *me*? Someone who served his country in the military? I began to feel a churning inside and a deeper conviction to stand up and make some positive changes, even if in just a small way.

After the fall break, I was eager to return to Western New England campus and continue my studies and public speaking and writing for the college paper. It felt good to be learning and sharing my thoughts and hopefully influencing others through my own personal, authentic perspective. It felt right to be speaking out against the war without pulling other individuals down. I didn't have a medal to throw into the river like Muhammad Ali, but I did have a voice, and I was using it to speak the truth as I saw it.

"Hey, man," I heard one evening, as I walked past a dorm room with its door wide open, "you're the guy who gave the antiwar speech, aren't you? And you write for the school paper too, right?"

I paused, took a few steps backward, and peered in.

"Yep, that's me," I said, to a tall, skinny, pale-skinned, hippie-looking guy standing next to what appeared to be an empty fish tank.

"Cool. Come on in. I've been wanting to talk with you." It was not so much an invitation as a soft command.

"I'm Tom," he quipped, offering his hand along with a big, warm smile, "and I'm really happy to meet you."

"Hey, Tom, I'm Larry," I said, shaking hands, a bit bewildered by his exuberant welcome. "It's nice to meet you too." Just then I noticed—amid the long, flowing hair, multiple strings of brightly colored love beads, and the pungent smell of patchouli oil—a good-sized boa constrictor wrapped around his neck.

"So, Larry," he continued matter-of-factly, though in a highly focused manner, "there's a lot you and I need to talk about. For starters, the whole spiritual awakening thing. I've been reading a lot about it, and I have a feeling you've had some experience with these kinds of things. Am I right?"

Where all of this was coming from I could only guess. As if he was reading my mind, he went on.

"I've overheard some of your conversations with other people on campus and put some of the pieces together. Obviously, you're not a regular student."

Well, I thought, that pretty much sums things up.

"And I'm not exactly your average Western New England student myself," he grinned, uncoiling the snake from around his neck and placing it into the glass cage.

"So, what would you like to talk about?" I asked with guarded fascination.

"Well," he began eagerly, "I had an amazing kind of experience from what felt like completely out of the blue. And I think it was some kind of spiritual awakening. Everything was filled with this indescribably beautiful light, calmness, and love. And I felt completely connected to the light, like it was part of me...or I was part of it. Nobody said anything. I mean, there wasn't some kind of booming voice from God, or whatever, but it felt—I don't know—holy, whatever that means. What's that all about?"

"Well, I'll be," I said, looking into his searching eyes. I felt my heart open with compassion. "I've got pretty much the exact same questions, Tom. I guess we do have a lot to talk about."

Over the coming months, along with getting to know each other and becoming good friends, we searched for, read, and discussed everything we could get our hands on to help explain the sense of spiritual awakening we'd both experienced. When we came across the teachings of Vedanta and the *Upanishads*, we learned they view the entire universe as a single conscious energy of which we are all a part. Bingo. That's it. That's what we had both experienced. We were especially excited to discover this reality of oneness could be experienced more consistently through the study and practice of meditation and yoga. It felt like we were exploring the next and deeper level of Western psychology, like classical physics and quantum physics describe the same universe, but from very different perspectives. In the same way that quantum physics takes a deeper dive into the mysteries of the universe, to me it felt like Eastern philosophies were helping me take a deeper dive into the mysteries of our very existence.

"Does this mean we have to become Hindus?" Tom asked one afternoon while we were discussing a book by Paramahamsa Yogananda called *Autobiography of a Yogi*.

"I hope not," I retorted. We both cracked up laughing, mostly because we didn't really know what a Hindu was.

"Okay, so where do you go to learn more about all this stuff?" Tom asked with impatience. "I mean, somebody's got to have some answers, right?"

The silence that followed felt both empty and pregnant with possibilities.

"I'm not sure, Tom," I responded, "but I like Yogananda's stories about his introduction to meditation and the spiritual life, and his meetings with some of the great sages who provided instructions and guidance on the path. I guess we just keep looking."

"Oh man," Tom added, "wouldn't it be cool to sit down and have a conversation with someone like that?"

"Yes, it would," I agreed. "That would be very cool."

A few nights later, I was studying some nineteenth-century lectures by William James, the father of American psychology, and was astonished to read:

> Ordinary consciousness is just one type of consciousness. Ordinary consciousness doesn't tell us the whole truth about the world. Mystical experiences are more intense states of consciousness in which a deeper and fuller reality is revealed... mystical states seem, to those who experience them, to be a form of knowledge.

"That's it!" I said out loud, and received a withering look over the top of the librarian's reading glasses. That's the perfect description of what we've been experiencing. It's the connection that's been there all along, and here's William James in the 1800s talking about this same stuff that we're experiencing.

In addition to these ongoing spiritual explorations during my first term at Western New England college, I was required to take a course in abnormal psychology. As the lectures and our readings on the various pathologies progressed, a disturbing, recurrent awareness of my own tendencies to identify with some of these psychological maladies became increasingly evident. Inner alarm bells began to sound. When I mentioned my plight to a few others after class, they were giddy with relief to hear they weren't alone in their concerns.

"Oh yes! I've been so depressed the last couple of weeks reading all this stuff."

"Yeh, my anxiety is keeping me up at night. I can barely sleep."

"I know, plus I'm having a lot of difficulty focusing on anything lately."

We looked around and found it hard to make eye contact with our other classmates without wondering about their state of mental health as well.

Back in my dorm room that night, I read about Freud's notion of "successful" psychotherapy being nothing more than "changing the extreme suffering of the neurotic into the normal misery of human existence." What? I thought. Is that the best we can hope for—normal misery?

It just didn't match up with my own experience. When I was drafted, my despair was crushing. All my dreams were dashed, and there appeared to be no way out. And yet, all those varied experiences in the army, both practical and mystical, had also taught me there are ways of thinking and being that produce insights and breakthroughs leading to new life possibilities.

That's it, I decided. I've been through military training with fierce drill sergeants preparing me for life-or-death situations. It was time to have a talk with my professor.

Next class period, I raised my hand and was called on.

"Professor, these symptoms are stated in such a way that most so-called normal people could be classified as showing signs of any number of diagnosable pathological behavior. They would therefore be classified as abnormal. Reading about them, I've been upset by feeling that way about myself."

He paused, reflected, and said, "Yes, to a degree, we all exhibit such symptoms."

I paused, and gathered my courage.

"But if that's the case, Professor, these symptoms would hold little or no effectiveness in distinguishing normal from abnormal behavior, and therefore would become useless as diagnostic tools."

There. I said it.

I waited for his response. My classmates waited. We listened as the clock in the back of the classroom ticked, ticked, ticked.

"Well," he said finally, with a casual shirk of his shoulders, "that's what the research indicates. Let's continue, shall we."

A drill sergeant he was not. I didn't doubt him. But I knew for certain that abnormal psychology was not going to be my thing. Yes, there's a need for that work to be done. But let someone else do it. I'm not pursuing a career in psychology based on such a limiting view of human potential—even if it is the most popular view in town.

I started looking at other fields of psychology with a more expansive view of human growth. Cognitive psychology, I learned, focuses on how people think, perceive, remember, and learn. Developmental psychology looks at human progression through various stages of life. Jungian psychology considers physical, emotional, social, and even spiritual aspects of human growth.

Educational psychology sounded especially interesting to me because it focuses on how people learn and retain knowledge in different ways. It was the very thing I was experiencing so powerfully in my own life. I was also drawn to social psychology because it includes the study of group processes, teams, and leadership—all things that had challenged me firsthand as an athlete and then again during my time in the army.

It boiled down to a simple choice for me. I could study mental diseases and limitations, or I could study branches of psychology capable of uplifting people, groups, and teams. I was growing eager to expand my horizons. Besides, I knew I could do with some upliftment of my own.

Fall semester came to a close, and the Mustang and I drove back to Neptune for the holidays. During my visit, I stopped by the local YMCA in search of a pickup game. Built in the 1920s in downtown Asbury Park, the old, four-story Y building was a throwback to a bygone era—including its residential rooms, lounges, locker rooms, a pool, and a basketball court. This was *not* a place that I had frequented, and I'd only set foot in the place once for a week-long summer swim class. I think I came closer to drowning than learning to swim. But it was freezing cold outside, and I was desperate to find a warm, dry place to play some quality ball. As I pushed open the heavy swinging doors and stuck my head in, my hope was to see some good pickup games in progress. I couldn't have been more disappointed. It was dinky, dingy, and dark. The walls were so close to the out-of-bounds lines, my first thought was, "Brace yourself for impact!" I knew it would be a crucial part of making a lay-up—and surviving.

The only action I encountered was a small cluster of young high school guys shooting around at the other end of the court. Oh well, I thought, nothing special going on here. Nevertheless, as always, it felt good to be on a basketball court. I started warming up, and one of the guys—a short stocky kid—walked over and introduced himself.

"Hi," he said, "I'm Bruce. We're trying to put a pickup game together, but we've got an odd number of players. Would you…," he started to say hesitantly, like he already knew what my answer would be, "do you wanna play with us?"

I hadn't played with high schoolers in a long while but… "Sure," I heard myself say, "let's give it a go."

"Great," he responded with a friendly smile. "We were really wanting to play, so we were glad when you walked in."

Bruce introduced me to the other guys, and as our game got underway, they seemed quite surprised and even impressed with my abilities. After a second game, I shared a little of my basketball story and asked about theirs.

"We're from Ocean Township High School," Bruce offered. "None of us play on the school team, though. We pretty much stick to pickup ball."

"Yeah," a tall guy said. "Me and Kanga are seniors. And these guys," he added, nodding toward the other three, "are juniors."

They all looked pretty young to me.

"So, who's Kanga?" I asked, a bit confused.

"Oh, that's me," Bruce answered.

"What?" the tall guy standing next to him chirped. "Didn't you see him jumping around out there?" With that he started bouncing the ball with both hands and hopping around the court with his feet together. Everybody cracked up.

Kanga organized a few more pickup games over the holiday break, and as we got to know each other on the court, we also connected as friends. That friendship led to expanding my experience of the world in a few unexpected ways.

During my spring semester, I took an economics class with a young and rather hip professor at Western New England named Rob. He seemed to know a lot about what was happening in the world and way more than just economics. He didn't make a big deal about it. In fact, he smiled a lot and was outwardly very easy going.

In addition to having me as a student in his class, he followed my editorials in the school paper and heard me speak at the various on-campus demonstrations. He was curious about my time in the army, what I learned there, and how it had impacted me.

"Reading your articles and listening to you speak, you obviously didn't choose to enlist in the army. What was it like for you? How did you survive those couple of years?"

A rush of emotions came flooding in. His questions struck a nerve.

"Getting drafted into the army was the lowest point in my life. All my hopes and dreams came crashing down, and I didn't know how to handle it. I was scared and angry, and disappointed with myself, all at the same time. For the first few weeks of basic training, there was just this complete feeling of helplessness."

"That's sounds really hard," Rob said. "How'd you get through it?"

"Well," I said, "part of it was what my drill sergeant called 'luck and destiny.' And he was right. My older brother insisted I take a typing class in high school, and that led to my assignment in personnel management. But that drill sergeant also provided an opportunity to find courage in myself that I didn't know was there. I realized I had to find some way to take some positive action in what I felt was a totally negative space. Otherwise, I'd just die inside before any bullet could ever get to me."

"So, what did you do?" Rob asked.

"The last place I wanted to be was in the army. But there I was, whether I liked it or not. So, I decided to work hard and do the best I could at whatever job they assigned me. I also knew that when I got out, I wanted to find a path that was right for me and to continue to do my best to make things better for others."

"Mm hmm," he responded with empathic approval. "I understand. And I applaud your desire to make a difference, Larry. In my college days, I was involved in quite a few demonstrations and protests of my own."

Something in the way he said those words led me to believe his involvement had been very intense. But there was no pretense, and he put me at ease. He encouraged me to continue speaking out about my beliefs and gave me some advice.

"You don't need to label yourself a radical, revolutionary, or anything else for that matter. It's not the label that makes a difference. Keep speaking and living the truth based on your own life experience. That will have the most impact."

He's been here, where I am now, I thought. He knows this path well and lives what he's teaching. I knew we'd be talking more and on a regular basis.

A few weeks later, he and his wife invited me for dinner. While we ate, I filled them in on my journey around sports, college, and the army. After dinner, he turned to the sizable elephant in the room.

"So, what are your plans for the future? I mean, are you planning to finish your degree here at Western New England?"

The look on his face shouted, "I sure hope not."

"Funny you should mention it," I said, a bit chagrined. "I'm aiming to transfer to the University of Michigan at the end of this school year."

"Wow," he exclaimed, beaming from ear to ear. "That's great, Larry. I went to Michigan! Tell me more. How'd you make your decision?"

"Well," I began, "I'm very interested in educational and social psychology, and Michigan has a world class Psychology Department. And Ann Arbor, by all accounts, is a very cool place in terms of political, social, music, arts, and countercultural activity. Plus, they have something new called the Residential College, or RC, which is one of the most innovative, interdisciplinary living and learning programs in the country. Plus, they have a great intercollegiate sports tradition. So, it sounds like just where I want to be, right?"

"Oh, man," Rob said, as he put his hands on his head and leaned back in his chair. "That's really fantastic, Larry. You'll get such a great education. And you'll have so much fun too. Plus, you'll have a lot more opportunities to connect with people who share your passions for civil rights, counterculture politics, the antiwar movement, and sports too."

"But," he added, with some gravity, "Michigan is a huge place. So, when you get to Ann Arbor, I want you to go see a mentor and trusted friend of mine. His name is Dick Mann. He's a psychology professor at U of M and a terrific person. Plus, he and his wife, Jean, teach in the Residential College. You'll like them. They're both very aligned to the things you talk and write about and to your whole approach of being the change you want to see. He'll explain how things work and can guide you through the whole process. Just tell him Rob sent you."

With Rob's guidance and blessing, I finished the year with confidence and was accepted into the University of Michigan for the coming fall semester.

I loaded up my things and drove the Mustang back home to Neptune to resume my summer job teaching math at the nearby Brookdale Community College. Over the summer, Kanga and I got reconnected again and enjoyed listening to music and playing regular pickup games around town together. About half way through the summer, we were hanging out one afternoon after a couple of games, and he asked if I wanted to come over to his place for dinner.

"Sure," I said, without much thought, "that'd be nice, thanks."

"Cool," he said, "I'll call my mom and let her know we're headed home."

Hmm, I wondered, is this a good idea? I knew he lived on the comfortable side of Asbury Park, in Ocean Township, and had at least one brother and a couple of younger sisters.

"But I don't want to impose on your family meal, man," I said.

"No problem, Larry," he assured me. "My mom is pretty laid back."

"What about your siblings? Won't they be kind of uncomfortable with this stranger just showing up on such short notice?" I asked.

"Well, maybe a little," he said with a sly grin. "But then, so was I, the first time I asked you to join our pickup game at the Y. I got over it, right? My family isn't racist. It's just that we don't live near any black people."

Fair enough, I thought. His parents and siblings were all friendly and curious. His house wasn't lavish or anything. Just very nice, in a simple way.

After dinner, we got to talking about our plans for the future.

"So, Kanga," I asked with sincere interest, "now that you've finished high school, what's next? Are you thinking about college?"

"Yes, I definitely am," he said with pride. "In fact, I've already been accepted."

"Cool," I said. "Around here?"

"Well, don't get me wrong," he answered, lowering his voice apologetically. "I mean, I grew up here. What's not to like about the Jersey Shore?"

"Okay," I said, thinking of several things. "But...?"

"Exactly," he said without taking a breath. "I gotta get out of here, man. I mean, I want to see what's happening outside this place. I want to know what other options are on offer, you know? I need to find out what life's all about. Does that make any sense?"

"Yes," I said, with empathy. "It makes a lot of sense. So, where are you going?"

"University of Michigan," he said with a big grin. "I'm gonna be in this really cool, experimental thing called the Residential College."

"Dude." My mouth dropped open. "You've got to be kidding me."

A few weeks before I headed off to school in Ann Arbor, I got a call from Kanga.

"Hello, this is Larry," I said, picking up the receiver on the second ring.

"Dude," he jumped in excitedly, "you are *not* going to believe what I just did."

"I can only imagine, Kanga," I answered, with a chuckle.

"I just got two tickets to see the Grateful Dead. *And* the Allman Brothers. *And* the Band."

"No way, man," I said with glee. "The Summer Jam thing up at Watkins Glen?"

"Yeah, dude," Kanga said, catching his breath. "That's what I'm saying. What do you think? Can you drive your Mustang? It's in upstate New York at that big Grand Prix race track up there."

"I hope. When is it?" I asked, with growing excitement.

"Saturday after next—July 28th."

"Cool," I said, "I'm in. Let's do it!"

After work, the following Friday, the trusty Mustang was once again packed—this time with camping gear and snacks —and early the next morning Kanga and I were happily truckin' on down the road, the Grateful Dead wailing mournfully from my eight-track player. We'd both missed out on Woodstock and felt lucky to be holding two of the hundred-and-fifty-thousand tickets that'd sold out in less than a day. After about four hours on the road, we got our first inkling that something was up at Watkins Glen.

"Larger-than-expected crowds continue to pour into the racetrack facility at Watkins Glen for the Summer Jam Festival," the radio DJ announced in a concerned tone. "Motorists are strongly advised to avoid the area."

"Hmm," I said, looking at Kanga. "Keep going?"

"We can't turn back now, man," he pleaded. "We're almost there, right?"

We passed a sign that read "Watkins Glen 20 Miles."

"Okay," I concurred, "let's do it," and continued on.

As we got closer, traffic slowed to a crawl. Up ahead were flashing lights and police barricades. Several cars in front of us took a right-hand turn and we followed. We took a left a few miles on, in hopes of inching closer to our common goal.

"The situation at Watkins Glen continues to deteriorate," the radio barked out its increasingly dire warnings. "The festival has been declared an emergency, and state officials are calling for water, food, and medical supplies to be flown in, in an effort to feed and take care of the steadily growing number of attendees."

I shot a dubious glance in Kanga's direction. He grinned, shrugged his shoulders, and pointed forward.

"Officials currently estimate the crowd size to be significantly bigger than the four hundred thousand people that attended the famed Woodstock outdoor festival in 1969. Tickets are no longer necessary. The gates are now open to everyone who is already on their way."

We soon entered a small hamlet, parked the Mustang on the side of the road, hoisted the camping gear onto our backs, and continued our adventure on foot.

"Is this crazy, or what?" he asked as an orange VW bus with peace signs painted on the sides pulled up alongside us as its sliding door rolled open. We were instantly met with a large cloud of pot smoke and an expanding wall of musical harmonies. A skinny guy with long curly hair, mirrored aviator sunglasses, and a tie-dyed bandana stuck his head out.

"Hey, dudes," he said with a grin. "You guys wanna ride with us?"

We looked at each other, hopped in, and happily wound our way down a series of back roads. The VW van was soon parked, and we found ourselves walking over torn-down fences into the concert grounds with our newly-found friends. Kanga and I picked out a spot on a little rise, pitched our tent, threw our stuff inside, and made our way up to the highest point on the site. I was keen to get a better view of the whole amazing happening going on around us. The immensity of the crowd was astounding. People and more people in every direction, as far as we could see—a giant ocean of humanity—all smiling and swaying to the sweet harmonies of the Grateful Dead.

As we watched in wonder, the wind shifted to our backs, and dark storm clouds rolled ominously in from the north. Their swift arrival was soon announced with three blinding flashes of lightning followed in quick succession by a series of long, loud crashes of thunder bouncing and echoing off the surrounding hillsides. Picking up speed, cooling gusts of wind began bending the pelting drops of falling rain sideways. The positive, highly-charged, magical energy of the occasion effortlessly spun the whirling rain into a wondrous vision of light and sound accompanied by uproarious laughter and dancing.

In the midst of the cavorting, three thoughts vied for my attention. First—as I recalled from some far distant science classes—lightning tends to strike the highest point. Secondly, that's exactly where we're standing. For miles in every direction, this is clearly the highest point. And thirdly, we *all* need to get moving, and quickly.

"Hey," I shouted to Kanga over the escalating roar of rain, wind, thunder, and music. "Kanga! We gotta get everyone off this hill, man. This is really dangerous!"

"Oh, really?" he asked, turning in my direction, as another blazing bolt of electricity leapt across the heavens above our heads. "Right," he yelled, as he jumped up, spun in midair, and unceremoniously took off downhill in a soggy kind of run.

As I watched him descend the slope, there was a sudden expansion in my consciousness encompassing all the people around me on the hilltop. Much like my experience in the army, this new awareness allowed me to abide in our complete oneness, while drawing my attention to a young man crouching down and in great distress. He was seemingly unable to move. As I walked over to check on him, he looked up. His eyes and trembling body were locked in darkening waves of fear and dread.

"Hey," I said, bending over and wrapping my arms around his shoulders, "we need to move, man." He looked at me blankly and said nothing. "It's not safe here," I heard my voice say softly inside the beautiful cocoon of peace we shared together. The swirling voices of panic and euphoria surrounding us gently faded into the background.

"Take my hand. I'll help you," continued my voice from some distant, though familiarly reassuring place. Two bodies in a single, comforting consciousness. Aware of the spinning world around us but no longer disturbed, the frightened young man slowly relaxed and even smiled as we safely made our way down the hill together.

What just happened? I wondered. I wasn't in the habit of throwing all caution to the wind, as we did that day. But the swirling elements carried a deeper message back to me: *Seek and you will find the peace that passes all understanding— even in the midst of the storm. We are all connected and worthy of love and respect, no matter the situation.*

8

A COMPLETE GAME CHANGER

I felt the lessons of this classroom experience seeping in deeply and knew this more aware way of thinking about and interacting with others was like a missing piece of the puzzle that had fallen into place for me.

By late August of 1973, I'd packed the trusty Mustang yet again and was headed out to start my third-and-a-half year of college. This time around, the journey included a ten-hour trek to the wilds of Michigan. My jitters were outweighed by a hopeful kind of anticipation of the possibilities awaiting me in Ann Arbor. Life was leading me toward a new beginning, but what was to come next was anyone's guess. About one thing, though, I was crystal clear: This is my decision and where I want to be. I am pursuing what inspires me, and what will hopefully prepare me for the next stage of my life.

Along with the excitement there was a pervasive and abiding sense of peace and wholeness that buoyed me as I made my way north. This heightened awareness and enjoyment of the beauty of life I attributed to my initial spiritual awakening in the army and my on-going encounters with the unity of all things. I wondered, though, how I would integrate my deep inner experiences with my day-to-day studies at Michigan.

As a youngster, home was the place I felt most rooted, connected, and accepted. I found my heart filled with a similar sense of belonging as I drove into Ann Arbor for the first time—like I was entering the place I would come to know as my second home.

To my eyes, Ann Arbor was a beautiful, bustling Midwestern college town, interwoven with a magically picturesque campus, quaint little shops and cafes, historic ivy-covered halls of learning, and a sprinkling of modern edifices. It was a living tapestry of past contributions, current relevance, and ardent hope for the future. The landscape and its people exuded a vibrant, positive kind of energy—a friendly "happening" kind of place—alive, comforting, and uplifting, all at the same time. Walking around campus, I was struck by how the students themselves looked so open, engaged, and even happy to be there. Wherever I went, I got, "Hey, man, what's happening? It's nice to meet you. Where're you from? Do you need help finding anything? It's easy to get lost on this campus." It made me feel welcomed and oddly expected, like I truly belonged.

In keeping with the unwavering encouragement I'd received from Rob—my mentor back at Western New England College—one of my first actions on campus was to seek out Dick Mann. I soon learned that as a member of the Psychology Department at U. of M., he was well-known and highly respected. I also learned he was currently en route to Ann Arbor from an extended sabbatical and was expected to return "soon."

I trusted Rob implicitly, but still, before I signed up for one of Professor Mann's courses, I decided to ask my student advisor about his teaching style and approach.

"So, Larry," she began, "what courses are you looking at this semester?"

"Well," I answered, pointing to my list of top choices, "I'm really interested in this Psychology 454 course on group dynamics offered by Professor Mann. What can you tell me about it? And him?"

"Oh, you'll just love Professor Mann and his courses," she said, without any hesitation. "But be prepared for something out of the ordinary. His approach is anything but traditional."

"What do you mean?" I wondered aloud.

"Well, they're quite different—his courses—and the way he teaches them too. 'Mind blowing,' is how I've heard more than a few students describe them. Mostly because his classes tend to challenge you as much personally as intellectually. It's hard to explain, but if you can get into one, which isn't easy, you'll get what I'm talking about."

Whoa, I thought, my time in the army was about as "personally challenged" as I'd ever like to be. But still, Rob was adamant I should try, so I thanked my advisor and tried to register for Professor Mann's group dynamics course.

As it turned out, Professor Mann's "Psych 454: Analysis of Interpersonal Behavior" course was a well-known and wildly popular 400-level course, technically only open to seniors and graduate students in the Psychology Department. Everyone, it seemed, wanted to get into that class. As a junior-level transfer student, my chances of getting in appeared slim at best, prompting me to feel some disappointment and annoyance. On the other hand, I figured, nothing ventured, nothing gained, and I began searching for a way forward. It was time, I decided, to meet this mystery man, Dick Mann, in person.

I found him locking his office door as he headed home for the day.

"Professor Mann," I blurted out in my excitement, "ah, hi, I'm Larry Holmes, and I'm not actually eligible to take your Psych 454 class, but I really want to, so I was hoping there was some way to be allowed to enroll in your class."

"Oh, hi, Larry," he responded quietly, turning around to give me his full attention. "It's great to meet you in person," he said, shaking my hand warmly.

"Rob called me over the summer and told me to expect you. And as for getting into the group dynamics class, I'm sure we can work it out. It's not so much an obstacle," he said, with a look of calm contentment, "as a minor inconvenience." His casual use of this phrase, like a mantra, caught my attention. It had the immediate effect of subtly changing my perspective.

On the first day of class, Professor Mann invited each of us to join him in a large circle of chairs he'd arranged "…just so we can see each other's faces more easily."

This is different, I thought. Plus, no desks, no blackboard at the front of the room, no front of the room. Just us looking at each other with a subtle feeling of discomfort as we each tried to settle into the unfamiliar arrangement.

After everyone was seated, amidst confused and concerned looks, he quietly said, "Welcome to this course in group dynamics. Throughout the semester, we'll be working together to study and analyze the behavior of individuals within various group settings, to gain insights into how these interactions impact each individual in the group, as well as the group as a whole. Let's get started today by going around the circle and having each person briefly introduce themselves."

We did, and once we'd all spoken, Professor Mann slowly looked around the circle but remained silent. Some of us began to fidget, but he just sat there while tension filled the room. Some heads were bowed. Others searched for eye contact.

I felt cornered. I didn't know where to look or what to do.

How do I behave? I wondered. What's my role? Should I say something? Who am I to say something, anyway?

The lack of direction made me feel helpless and confused. It reminded me of the time I rode the bus to basic training with my fellow army recruits. None of the normal outlets of small talk or joking around felt appropriate. Intuitively, I sensed it would help if we could share our feelings with each other. But how? So, there we sat, looking at each other, and then at him, and then back at each other. Slowly, the questions came...

"Professor Mann, what are we going to study?" the guy next to me asked. "I mean, is there an outline or curriculum for the course?"

"We will explore the dynamics of the group process," he said with a warm smile. "There's no set curriculum. It will develop as we get to know each other and the group."

"What textbook will we be using?" another classmate asked.

"There is no textbook," he said, and was met with quizzical looks.

Another long silence followed. And then another volley of questions.

"Professor Mann, how do you define group dynamics?" someone asked.

"Well," he said, "the dynamics of a group are what happens among all the members in the group."

"Professor, your course description includes the words "effective group process." What does that mean, exactly?" another classmate asked.

"Effective group process facilitates the group's purpose and goals," he offered. "Group process," he added, leaning in and looking around the circle, "is exactly what's happening here right now. *We* are the group. Whatever you say or do, and how you say and do it—and what you don't do or say, for that matter—all of this is creating the content and the dynamics of the group. This is precisely the process we will be studying."

He stopped short of addressing the elephant in the room: How do we do that? And for some of us, the even bigger question, "What the hell is this course even about? No textbook. No explanation or directions on how to behave. Not even a clear goal."

The tension was thick and proceeded to thicken—all of us stuck on some kind of merry-go-round, searching for a ticket to a not-yet-defined destination. Again and again, we returned to where we'd begun—questions and more questions—followed by what felt like veiled responses.

Underneath it all, I tried to identify my feelings—stuck, frustrated, helpless, annoyed. Maybe even disappointed? So, what's up with his unwillingness to relieve our confusion? Why doesn't he at least give us a hint? That's silly—of course there's a purpose to all this. But damned if I know what it is.

Or, I thought, what if Professor Mann actually *wants* us to feel uncomfortable? Maybe he's trying to teach us something? I guess I should say something. Or maybe I should wait—for what?—until I have something worthwhile to say. What's the sense of disturbing or influencing the group process until I have something valuable to share? You know—"create no bad karma."

Time stood still as we waded through what felt like emotional quicksand.

"People seem hesitant to speak," he stated calmly, as the class period ended. "What's going on for you? What are you feeling?"

"Uncomfortable," one young woman offered, clearly sugar-coating her more visceral feelings.

"Yeah," others nodded in agreement.

"Okay," he said with enthusiasm. "Now that's some helpful input you've added to our group dynamics. Why are you feeling that way? What's your discomfort about? Give it some thought, people, and we'll discuss your responses next time we meet."

There was quite a buzz as we filed out of the classroom together, and not much of it was uplifting.

"What the hell was that all about, anyway? I am totally frustrated," one guy blurted out in the hallway.

"Yeah," another added, "I have no idea what this course is even about."

"I thought it was kind of interesting," someone offered, in a faint attempt to say something positive.

"Yeah, but where's it going? I'm thinking I might drop this course while I can."

"Will there be exams? Or papers? He never really said, did he?"

"Should we be taking notes? I mean, I'm not sure what I'd even write down."

I wandered back to my room in a daze and plopped onto the bed. I felt unsure of myself and uncomfortably out of my depth. Who am I to speak up anyway? This whole class is a bunch of very smart seniors and graduate students. I'm the only junior.

My head and heart were awash in a swirling tide of thoughts and feelings. How did I deal with all the difficult interactions with my teammates and coaches on the basketball court? What gave me the courage to face all the daily challenges in the army—and some very scary drill sergeants? What's holding me back? Why all the hesitation?

I wondered, what if I'm not smart enough or good enough to succeed here?

Yeah, I thought, what if I'm just not capable of succeeding at a place like this? Western New England is one thing. But this is the University of Michigan—the big leagues—and these are some very bright, well-educated, upper middle-class, high achievers on the fast track to…

"Whoa, Larry," I could hear my brother, Al Junior, saying to me. "Calm down. Don't doubt yourself now. You've overcome so many obstacles and difficult situations. Remember those times and keep moving forward."

"Don't think about crashing!" Isn't that what Lieutenant Bates shouted out while flying a helicopter at three thousand feet with a giant grin on his face? "Just focus on the task at hand—flying! You'll be fine."

So how, I wondered, do I take all this and apply it to Psych 454? How can I—an introvert's introvert—successfully participate in a class like this? What am I missing?

"Forget about all the guys that are trying to tear you down," Henry advised me more than once. "Look for the people that are lifting you up and bringing you light."

Okay. So how can I make a positive contribution in what feels like a very challenging situation? What kind of light can I bring?

And then—Bingo! It came to me—What's the purpose of our group as a whole? That's the question we need to ask ourselves. Our way out of this rabbit hole.

"Okay, folks, why were some of you feeling so uncomfortable during our last class period?" Professor Mann began. "Let's talk about that. What was going on for you?"

"Well," one of our classmates began, "we clearly weren't making much progress. I think we need clearer instructions from the leader to help us in this group process."

Others nodded in agreement or added their own take on our need for better leadership to move forward.

Then I heard my name.

"Hey, Larry," one of my classmates across the circle said, "you're pretty quiet. What are you thinking over there?"

Caught in the act. Emerging from my private reverie, I saw that everyone was looking at me. Uh oh, I thought.

"I'm not sure," I said, feeling in the spotlight, undressed, and alone on stage.

A little corner of my mind was slowly illuminated, helping me connect with what I knew to be true for me, and I mustered the courage to share it with my classmates.

"I'm here," I started, "because I heard this course could be a great way to learn more about myself and about the group process too. But I'm a junior transfer student into the Residential College, and I had to ask for special permission to enroll in this senior-level class. So, here I am, and honestly, it's a really uncomfortable situation for me. Mostly," I continued, looking around the circle, "because it's really challenging for me to find the authority to speak up— as an underclassman—in this class. So, I'm experiencing all of those things right now."

The whole circle lit up with smiles and even some chuckles, and slowly others began to share what was going on for them.

"Last week I felt really disappointed," someone offered, "mostly with the lack of structure or content. I wanted—really—I *expected* more of both."

"Yeah, me too," another added.

I felt like I was trying to climb a mountain in the dark and wasn't at all sure of my footing. What's the next step we should take? And what happens if we take it?

From deep inside, I felt a surge of the self-empowerment I discovered leading a platoon in the army.

"Maybe," I said slowly, "it's not so much about what Professor Mann wants. What if it's up to us to determine what we want to explore in these group sessions? Maybe that's why he isn't saying much right now?" I suggested, as we all looked his way.

He offered the class a bemused grin. Nothing more.

There was a general raising of eyebrows. nodding of heads, and shrugging of shoulders, followed by a deafening silence, as everyone turned back—in *my* direction.

Hmm, I wondered, where am I going with this? I wasn't sure.

"Look," I heard myself saying, "I don't have a lot of answers—mostly just questions—but I don't think we're here just to follow directions or orders, even from Professor Mann. I guess what I've been wondering is—without genuine, open participation from me—from each of us—how can our group ever move forward? Don't we all need to find a way to contribute...in whatever way we can? Then we might learn something about how groups and social systems really function. And isn't that the purpose of our being here in this class...to experience and understand more about group dynamics? Not theoretically, but in real life? This is our group. We have to take care of it." There. I said it, and the world didn't collapse. And I felt more like I was being myself. My best self. No nonsense. Just puttin' it out there.

More silence. Then a few low mumblings and the beginnings of opinions shared with nearby neighbors. And with that, instead of complaining about our discomfort, we slowly and awkwardly began discussing the purpose of our group.

Over the coming weeks, we discovered that in addition to dealing with countless external processes, our internal beliefs, assumptions, and values were affecting our thoughts, feelings, and interactions with one another in subtle but profound ways.

At first, we found it a very uncomfortable experience. Someone would start to make a point or support a notion and, "Wait. What?" someone else would respond. "Are you saying you believe that? 'Cause that's not really been my experience at all." And off we'd go in a new direction, checking our assumptions and comparing our experiences. We found it immensely helpful to laugh at ourselves and the variety of quirks and biases we each brought to the table. Through trial and error, we discovered the value of trusting the good will of our classmates and working together to forge a common framework of values for our group as a whole.

Along the way, we realized it was very important to pay close attention to what everyone was saying—and in particular, to what everyone was *meaning*. It was the only way we could figure out how to really understand—and in turn, truly honor—each other. It wasn't easy. And it wasn't without some loud disagreements. But we were slowly crafting a process of our own design and the group was becoming *ours*, not Professor Mann's.

As we continued our group dynamics journey together, we often found ourselves taking a few precarious steps forward, only to then take a few steps backward. When one of us got frustrated with the process, Professor Mann gently guided us back.

"I don't get what this is all about," someone would say in an exasperated tone. "I mean, it's interesting and all, but are we really learning anything?"

"Ah," Professor Mann would perk up, and offer a clarifying question. "What is it that you would most like to learn about group processes? What do you want to say to the class about that? How would you all like to proceed?"

Though uncomfortable, we steadily learned to speak into the group with the intention of finding useful answers to our questions, without throwing the learning process back onto Professor Mann. The key, we discovered, was to work out the next step, not the entire journey. Gradually we began taking more ownership of our own education and learning. It was a heady and somewhat mind-boggling experience. I came to see the most important thing was to engage in a positive, wholehearted way, based on my values, beliefs, best intentions, and inherent connection with others. And not to worry about failing.

By mostly staying out of the way, Professor Mann showed us another way to get to the real heart and purpose of the group process. Not by giving lectures and presenting theories. Instead, he carefully fostered a safe, human laboratory to help each of us become more aware of how our comments, emotional outbursts, and even our silences have a real impact on individual members and the group as a whole. He may have been educated at Harvard and Michigan, two highly traditional universities, but Professor Mann certainly wasn't a traditional academician. His unique teaching style provided the fertile ground we needed to discern the intricate patterns and processes of personal growth happening in our group and enabled us to discover why and where we wanted to go, how we might get there, and who we hoped to become as we traveled together.

Sometimes—in sports, or business, or life—there's a particular moment or happening when the momentum appears to shift in a new direction. Such game changers often spark dramatic transformations, insights, and whole new ways of looking at the world. I sensed that taking Professor Mann's Psych 454: Analysis of Interpersonal Behavior course was exactly that for me—as if I'd landed on another planet—and life would never be the same, in an extraordinarily good kind of way.

I felt the lessons of this classroom experience seeping in deeply and knew this more aware way of thinking about and interacting with others was like a missing piece of the puzzle that had happily fallen into place for me. How, I wondered, could this respectful, compassionate approach to relationship building be used not just in a small group setting but to solve our bigger social, racial, and political challenges? Clearly the world is vastly more complex than our classroom experiment, but change has to start somewhere, right?

Both inside and outside the classroom, Professor Mann maintained a soft-spoken and unassuming manner. He wasn't boisterous or dramatic, and unlike some professors who seemed to be in constant teaching mode, he was genuinely more interested in what other people had to say than he was in his own opinions. For being such a well-known and highly respected professor, he always seemed to have plenty of time to listen. When we bumped into each other on campus or around the Residential College, we always enjoyed an uplifting conversation about education, politics, sports, spirituality, or whatever topics happened to be on our minds.

"How are you, Larry?" was his usual first question, followed by his rapt attention to whatever I had to say. Over the coming months and years, he concluded each of these impromptu meetings by sincerely asking me, "Do you need help with anything, Larry?" With utmost care—as if he were using some kind of secret radar—he would pick up on the subtle nuances of what I was saying, ask a few insightful questions, and more often than not, help me figure out whatever I was wrestling with at the moment. I often wondered, How does he do that?

After class one day, Professor Mann pulled me aside and offered a surprising invitation.

"Hey, Larry, how'd you like to walk home with me for a cup of tea and a chat? I'd like you to meet my wife. You'll love Jean. She teaches in the Residential College too."

"Really?" I said, as my eyebrows met the rim of my hat.

"Oh, yeah," he chuckled, "you're famous around our place. Our kids want to know who this Larry guy is, and Jean's been especially eager to meet you. Plus, she's got a cool idea for a new course she wants to discuss." He grinned in my direction.

"Okay," I said, a bit dumbfounded. That's kind of surprising, I thought.

The Manns' home was simple, with a warm, lived-in feel. Jean welcomed me in with a friendly wave of her hand and a smile, while she deftly hung my coat and scarf on a peg behind the front door.

"Just slip your shoes off here, Larry, and you can put these on," she said, matter-of-factly, offering me a wooly pair of house slippers from the shelf behind the door.

"Come on in," Professor Mann said, showing me into a cozy living room with an inviting sofa, colorful chairs, an enormous stone fireplace, and a wonderfully wide assortment of books lining the walls.

"Make yourself at home," Jean added, "and I'll put the kettle on."

"Do I smell cookies?" Professor Mann asked with keen interest as they both disappeared into the kitchen.

I eagerly perused their eclectic collection of books and family photos.

"Find anything interesting?" Professor Mann asked, as they returned with trays of tea and goodies and set them on the coffee table.

"You have a lot of great books, Professor Mann," I said with genuine delight.

"Yeah, we've collected a few over the years," he said with a chuckle. "We'll show you around later; they're all over the place, really—upstairs, downstairs—you name it. Oh, and please just call us Dick and Jean, okay?"

I settled into one of their cozy armchairs as they claimed spots on the sofa across from me. Jean poured out our tea and offered us still-warm cookies.

"So, Larry," Dick began, "tell us about yourself. You're an older student so I imagine you've had some interesting times getting here. We're all ears."

And just like that, my story—with all its various ups and downs—came tumbling out in a cascade of recollections. Their keen interest and calm presence encouraged me to share deeply. Their thoughtful questions allowed me to respond with surprising clarity and led me to helpful insights about my life experience.

"Wow," Dick exclaimed, "that's quite a journey. How have all these situations and circumstances impacted you? What have you been learning?"

"Well," I began slowly, sipping my tea, "mostly, they've challenged me to grow up and take responsibility for my life. To make a conscious stand for the truth, as I see it."

"Yes, indeed. Wonderful," he said with a warm smile. "These days, those are not the typical experiences that undergrad students have had *before* coming to college."

"We can really relate to your feelings of wanting to change things for the better," Jean offered quietly. "Especially with three young boys to raise, we're very concerned about what and how they're learning, and the kind of country they're growing up in."

"Mm-hmm," Dick agreed, "and just providing information isn't enough. As educators, Jean and I have come to see how important it is to stimulate deeper thinking and provide experiences that promote personal growth. Otherwise, students remain comfortable and stuck in old mindsets."

"Ah," I said, as I took in what they were saying. "Psych 454. Group dynamics."

"Precisely," Dick grinned.

"And we've been quite involved in a variety of social, political, and educational change efforts," Jean added with excitement, "starting back at Harvard—and more recently, here in Ann Arbor. Our work in getting the Residential College up and running is one example."

"And," Dick added, "we were very involved in organizing and running the antiwar teach-ins here on campus a few years ago."

Before I knew it, the two of them were off and running —telling story after amazing story of their past and ongoing efforts to expand their own awareness, and to be and encourage the change they hoped to see in the world.

"Straight, with no chaser" was the phrase that came to my mind, as they openly shared their hopes, dreams, joys, and sorrows in a free-flowing, unedited fashion. We talked, laughed, and cried together as the afternoon swung gently into evening.

It all felt quite natural and right—just what good friends would do for one another—have a cup of tea and a long, heart-felt chat. Their kind hospitality, offered with such ease and lack of pretense, assured me I was seen and valued, and most of all, was free to be myself. It was a simple, profound, and uplifting experience, and the beginning of a life-long friendship with two very experienced and wise mentors.

Wow, I thought, as I walked home. That was some cup of tea.

9

POSSIBILITIES

Based on our beliefs and best intentions, our daily lives became the proving ground of our developing convictions, and in the process, we discovered an inherent, loving connection with one another.

Housed in the East Quadrangle Dormitory, the Residential College—RC for short—was designed as a living-learning experiment in interdisciplinary learning, community engagement, and social action. The blending of living quarters with classrooms, faculty offices, common rooms, studios, performance spaces, a cafeteria, and a library provided regular interactions among students and faculty and forged a powerful community of friendships and solidarities. I loved the whole approach and setup. East Quad was our self-contained internal campus within the larger external campus. In the bone-numbing chill of Michigan winters, it was pure luxury not having to leave the dorm, except for the odd exploration of downtown shops and cafes, concerts, sporting events, or peaceful walks in the nearby arboretum we affectionately dubbed the "Arb."

RC classes were small and informal, and in our common search for a better way to learn, no stone—philosophical, political, social, or cultural—was left unturned or unchallenged. Poetry provided a unique lens into the study of immigration issues. Videography enabled us to document and carefully study the oral histories of local townspeople in the far north of Michigan's Upper Peninsula. In urban studies, we assisted with efforts to re-acclimate former inmates after their release from the infamous Detroit prison system. For the most part, I found this kind of head-on, whole-person way of engaging in the learning process far more beneficial, fulfilling, and productive than the traditional academic approach of attending lectures, taking tests, and writing papers. I'd come a long way since those early years in my 'hood, and I felt grateful to be in such an uplifting and nourishing learning environment.

On the other hand, this experiential approach to education came with a regular dose of challenges that required me to get outside my comfort zone. Beyond the demands of learning at the collegiate level, our professors provided a steady stream of opportunities for the relentless exploration of pressing social issues and dilemmas, and in turn, the careful consideration of our own personal perspectives, beliefs, and biases as well as those of our classmates, professors, and guest presenters.

"What do you think about this issue, folks?" I heard our professor ask in class one day.

Uh-oh, I thought. What do I think? Our entire class was engaged in a heated debate about the use of marijuana on campus and in the larger community of Ann Arbor as a whole. A few in our group thought it a good thing that dope was considered illegal.

"Well," one guy argued, "aside from the undeniably relaxing and mind-altering effects of the direct experience of having a toke, what I've been reading says it leads to the use and abuse of other more dangerous drugs."

"Not necessarily," someone else offered. "To me it's more like alcohol. I mean, what's the difference? You get drunk. You get high…"

"You get drunk *and* high," a girl added, to the group's general amusement.

"See, that's my point. One thing leads to another. That's why we had the prohibition against alcohol in the first place. So many people were suffering from alcoholism and all the dysfunction it was causing in American families, the Federal government had to step in and do something."

"Yeah," another guy retorted, "but prohibition ended like a thousand years ago."

More laughter.

"Yeah, all we're saying is, make it legal—you know, like alcohol is."

And on and on it went.

"Okay," our professor announced, at the end of class, "that was a great discussion, everyone. And to that *last* point, if you're really interested in finding a solution to this problem, I'd like you all to attend the Ann Arbor City Council meetings throughout the semester. You can continue this discussion and also hear what council members and other adult members of the community think. They meet the first Thursday of each month, so this Thursday is their next meeting. They start at 7:00 p.m. at City Hall, which is just a few blocks away. This will be your main project for this semester, so I'll expect you to report back on the discussions and the final resolution. Any questions?"

Yes, I thought. Really? I'd never even imagined attending a city council meeting, and I was skeptical this particular class assignment would yield much in the way of a worthwhile learning experience. For one thing, who's going to listen to students at a town council meeting? And second, I was pretty sure I knew what kind of things were discussed and decided on in places like that. I'd grown up hearing stories about politics and politicians whose primary interest was satisfying their usually well-to-do supporters. It certainly didn't seem like a place where significant change could happen or even be discussed. In my mind, I wasn't likely to learn much of any value and figured it would just be a big waste of time.

"I'm not studying political science," I informed my professor as my classmates filed out. "I don't really have much interest in the formal political system. Could I skip those meetings and choose something else to study for my project?"

"I think you might find it a very educational experience, Larry," she offered with a smile. "Maybe even invigorating."

I considered her claim but couldn't really imagine it playing out like that.

"Politics aren't really my thing," I said, in a last-ditch effort to persuade her.

But there she sat, grinning, like a Cheshire cat. She tilted her head to one side and blinked pleasantly.

"Okay," I said, surrendering to her encouragement, "I'll give it a go."

The next Thursday, I found myself dutifully climbing the broad marble steps and entering through the heavy front doors of City Hall. I wondered what I was letting myself in for. Once inside, however, I was pleasantly surprised to see so many different kinds of people hanging out together—young and old, suits and jeans, long hair and short. The place was packed.

"Hi, I don't think we've met," an older gentleman said, turning in my direction.

"It's my first city council meeting," I said softly.

"Welcome," he responded warmly, offering his hand. "I'm Bob. It's great that you came. We always need more people involved to keep things moving along."

"Nice to meet you," I said, shaking his hand. "I'm Larry. I'm here with my class."

"Ah, I figured," he nodded, pulling on his large gray beard. "I was just chatting with your professor over there. We're both regulars at these things. She says you all are having some lively discussions about one of the items on tonight's agenda."

"Really?" I asked.

"Yeah, it's an on-going debate, really," he explained. "The Board's considering a proposal to legalize marijuana in Ann Arbor. Or at least to make it more like receiving a parking ticket instead of a criminal offense, like it is now. Feel free to add your voice to the mix. We need all the support we can get."

Hmm, I thought, didn't see that coming. Still, I was surprised at the good vibes being offered in such a formal and unfamiliar setting.

The meeting was called to order, and I was genuinely amazed to see how engaged and eager everyone was to discuss issues and share their questions, concerns, and opinions. I'd had plenty of intense discussions with my friends and fellow students, but that was just us. This local government thing felt like the real deal. I felt hopeful to see that something might actually get changed for the better. I had to admit my professor was right. In Ann Arbor, at least, city council meetings are lively, even invigorating events.

Over the coming months, I grew more familiar, and to some degree, more comfortable with the local, grass-roots political scene in Ann Arbor. To my surprise, it was a public stage that appeared open to everyone—rich or poor, tall or short, male or female, black or white—if you were game enough to enter the fray. I felt a whole new set of possibilities opening, and slowly, I began to step into the arena, risk disagreement and criticism, and add my voice in support of what I hoped was for the good of the whole.

During a particularly heated council meeting focused on the on-going debate about whether to decriminalize the possession of small amounts of marijuana, I felt the urge to speak. As I made my way toward the microphone, I got some thumbs-up from my classmates.

"This," I began, looking toward the city council members, "is an issue of special concern for the young and disadvantaged in our community."

"That's right," someone from the crowd added, in support of my statement. I smiled. It made me feel like my point was being understood and encouraged me to forge ahead.

"I think we should change our city's regulations in line with the proposal, so we no longer taint young people's lives by convicting them of a serious crime for possession of a few joints—less than an ounce. If it's for their own personal use, who are they actually harming? Our police officers could focus more on serious crimes. And wouldn't that be better for our whole community?"

I didn't know if what I said was completely correct from a legal perspective, but I was moved to share my viewpoint. Afterwards, I had a deja vu moment when three very well-known local radicals, and obvious users, approached me.

"Way to go, man," one of them said, reaching out his hand to shake mine. "That was awesome. We really appreciate what you had to say."

"Yeah," another chimed in, "and I think the city council did too."

"Great job, man," the third added. "We were just talking, and we wondered if you'd like to join our efforts with the counterculture movement here in Ann Arbor? We could really use your perspective and your voice."

Their appreciation was nice and affirming, but some inner tension made me hesitate, and I realized it was definitely not the personal accolades I was seeking. It was something deeper. What was it?

"Thanks, that's kind of you," I said. "I appreciate your encouragement. And thanks for your invitation too. I've got a lot on my plate right now with classes and a community service project I'm working on down in Detroit. Let me think about it."

Civil rights and antiwar demonstrations were happening all across America, and I was sincerely interested in finding some role I could play moving forward. But I was also having some real trouble reconciling myself with the more radical aspirations and violent tactics of some groups. In my heart of hearts, I felt it was more about treating everyone with dignity and respect, regardless of our external differences or beliefs. Besides, I thought, as I walked back to the dorm with my classmates, I don't need to label myself a radical or a revolutionary. I just need to keep speaking the truth from my own life experience. Who knows, maybe sharing my point of view at a public meeting is a step in the right direction?

Ann Arbor, and the Residential College in particular, provided me with an up-close and personal glimpse into what I thought of as the "haves" of American society. As far back as high school, I'd wondered what was being discussed around the dinner table of families different from my own. What did they honestly think about the state of affairs in our communities and in the country as a whole? For sure, some of my friends and classmates took what they had for granted. But most were friendly, authentic, and deeply caring people. As our conversations and friendships deepened, I also came to see they were often just as dissatisfied as I was about how things in our country were going and equally confused about how we could live in a way that was more authentic, and truer to our ideals and values.

One of my close female friends and romantic interests in the RC was a lovely girl named Mary. From our first meeting in class, we just seemed to click and soon started hanging out, taking walks in the Arb on Saturday afternoons, and getting to know one another. From an external point of view, we were a pretty unlikely match in some ways. She came from a wealthy suburb of Detroit—home to senior executives from the big three car manufacturers. But despite Mary's upper-class upbringing, or maybe because of it, she was aware of a lot of things in society that needed to be changed, and that somehow added to our chemistry.

"When I watch the news," she began, on one of our afternoon walks, "it makes me sad to see how unfairly so many people are treated. And how they're judged for trying to make things better. It just seems so wrong."

"Yeah," I said, "it's a difficult situation for a lot of people."

"What was it like for you, Larry?" she asked. "I mean, was it dangerous where you grew up?"

"Yeah, it *was* dangerous," I said, searching for words to capture my inner and outer experience. "But more so if you weren't a part of the neighborhood. The most danger came when you were careless enough to venture outside of your 'hood."

"Why?" she asked. "I'm not sure I understand."

"Well," I explained, "everyone knew who belonged and who didn't. And if you found yourself somewhere you didn't belong, you could be in some real trouble."

"Wow," she said. "That's pretty scary."

I told her about the fight and the guy with a gun after the Freehold basketball game when I was in high school, and how well the movie *West Side Story* captured my experience growing up.

"It's hard to imagine being constantly on edge like that," she said, giving my hand a squeeze. "Living with so much uncertainty and fear all the time."

"When it's your everyday experience," I tried to explain, "your main focus is on what you have to do to survive. It's just part of your life, and you share the experience with your friends and family. Sometimes, like on the team bus, you even laugh with friends about it. Otherwise, it can be too much." I noticed that even telling the story made me chuckle a bit.

"I knew it wasn't right," I continued, "and at some point, I guess by the time I graduated from high school, maybe, I realized the bigger danger was actually settling for the comfort of the known and familiar."

"What do you mean?" she asked.

"Well, it's an irrational kind of fear of the outside world —whether it's real or imagined. It was a constant factor when I was growing up. But eventually, I decided I just didn't want to live like that anymore. I guess because it felt like such a dead-end kind of mindset. So, here I am, a long way from home, loving being with you and my other friends here in the RC."

"I'm glad you're here," she said. "It must be hard though?"

"Oh, sometimes," I reflected. "But then I remember all the differences are not necessarily bad or a barrier to interacting with someone who has grown up in another place with a different set of challenges. Though it definitely takes a kind of openness and patience, without judging other people's life experience. If that makes any sense?"

"It does," she said with a smile. "It's a lot to take in."

Another of my close friends was Andy from the comfortable side of the tracks in Silver Springs, Maryland. His small frame and penchant for staying up late quickly earned him the nickname Roach.

"Hi, Larry. It's great to meet you," he said, the first time we met, with what sounded like almost a giggle of delight. He shook my hand vigorously and looked at me with a bright and genuinely warm smile. "I'm really looking forward to being here and experiencing all of what the RC has to offer."

Honestly? I thought. He's very exuberant. Maybe he's high or something?

"What are you studying, Larry?" he asked earnestly.

"Well, right now I'm leaning toward social and educational psychology," I answered. "How 'bout you?"

"Oh, I'm in that new six-year pre-med program," he offered matter-of-factly.

"Whoa," I responded, "I guess we won't be seeing much of you around here."

In no time, I learned our out-of-the ordinary introduction was, in truth, Roach's authentic, open-hearted welcome to everyone he met. It's just who he was, and we all loved him for it. Until Roach showed up, I'd assumed there were two basic types of students in Ann Arbor: those focused on academics and getting ahead, and those who—along with their academic goals—were keen on pursuing a counterculture lifestyle, social justice, racial equality, and perhaps some interest in spiritual matters. Roach soon blew these little boxes out of the water by joining in our regular, late-night parties with enthusiasm. In the process, he also revealed what felt like a super-power to the rest of us, his uncanny ability to party deep into the night, straggle home, crack open his books, and nonchalantly put in two or three solid hours of legitimate study. None of us could fathom how he managed this feat on such a regular basis. All we could do was shake our heads in wonderment.

"Dude, what are you doing? Turn out the light. Go to bed."

"I can't," he retorted with his perpetual smile. "I have a chemistry test in a few hours. I gotta study."

"Roach," we wailed in unison. "Just go to bed, man."

Roach's intense pursuit of his pre-medical studies was uniquely balanced with his deep appreciation for the beauty and wonder of nature and his unwavering interest in the spiritual meaning of life.

"They're all part of the same thing," he offered, when we asked him about his wide range of passions. "Science explores the world around us. Medicine explores the human body. And when we get high or take psychedelics or meditate, we're exploring our minds and inner experiences. They're all just part of the same, big, beautiful thing. You're doing it through the body or the spirit. Either way, I want to be a part of it."

I watched one night as Roach was drawn into a deep kind of inner reverie. He caught my glance and grinned, "So, Larry, I'm experiencing a really intense kind of tingling in the space between my eyebrows. What's that all about? Should I be worried?"

Roach and I had talked about my own on-going spiritual experiences and discussed some of the many and varied books I'd read to help me understand these experiences and integrate them into my life. I'd introduced him to some of my favorites including *Be Here Now* by Ram Dass, *Autobiography of a Yogi* by Swami Yogananda, *Patanjali's Yoga Sutras*, written by someone named Patanjali, I reasoned, and the Indian scriptures known as *The Upanishads*.

"No problem, Roach," I assured him. "The place between your eyes is called the third eye. It's one of the higher energy centers in the body. Activity there is considered a very positive thing on the spiritual path."

"Aah, that's good to know," he said, "because now I'm seeing a giant, glimmering ocean of bright, blue light dancing all around and inside that space between my eyes."

"Cool, I've read about that too," I assured him. "It's actually considered a really good thing."

"Whoa," he said a few minutes later. "Now the blue light—all of it is being condensed into a sparkling blue diamond. Am I still good, Larry?"

"Oh yeah," I answered. "For really serious practitioners of meditation, a vision of the pearl of blue light is fervently sought after. It's seen as an indication of significant progress on the inner spiritual journey."

"Oh," he said quietly. "That's nice. It's very beautiful."

That's how it was with Roach. He slipped seamlessly between his intense exploration of medicine and the human body, and the structures and mysteries of nature and the universe and took them all in stride.

Michael was one of Roach's closest East Coast friends, a soft-spoken guy with an air of seriousness about him. Meeting Michael was like bumping into a soft cloud. He had a full, unmistakable kind of presence about him but no hard edges you could put your finger on. He arrived in the RC with the extraordinarily apt nickname of "Mouse," and we soon bonded over our common love of basketball.

"Hey, Larry, you wanna play some pickup ball?" he asked, on a regular basis. It was music to my ears to have a friend who loved the game as much as I did, and he was a good player too. We got to enjoy hanging out together before and after our games, and it became abundantly clear he intended to make significant changes in the largely working-class neighborhoods he came from.

"There's a lot that needs to be improved for the average person," he offered one evening, while we were cooling down and talking about our after-college intentions. "It shouldn't be that hard to change things, right? We just need to determine a better, more equal way of doing things and slicing up the pie. If we stick together and keep at it, it should work, right?"

"Those are some lofty goals, Mouse," I responded. "But —to be honest—how would you rate your chances of success?"

"It's work that needs to be done, Larry," he stated calmly but with sincere conviction. "People deserve a better deal in this world. First, we need to agree on what that looks like. Then the work starts. But if we don't all play our part, how will it ever happen? I came to Ann Arbor to learn what I need to know to be able to do what I can."

Pure Mouse. As a deeply passionate, and natural-born student of labor relations, Mouse was forever of and for the equality of every man, woman, and child. When, on occasion, he did speak up, it was always with a grounded kind of certainty about the immense value of *all* human beings. He sincerely intended to do his part to make a real difference in the lives of working-class people.

"Hey, guys, let's go to the Arb," Roach suggested playfully one cold, winter afternoon. A bunch of us were hanging out together, mostly commiserating with one another about how much homework we had to do and how little we felt like doing it.

"What?" Mouse said with cautious alarm. "It's freezing out there, dude."

"Yeah, Roach," I added, "and there's like six inches of snow on the ground."

"Come on," Roach implored. "The arboretum's beautiful this time of year."

"Plus," offered Kanga, looking out the window, "there's still some daylight left."

"Okay," I said, "let's do it."

With that, we were soon covered head to toe in winter garb and joyfully laden with various thermoses of hot chocolate, bottles of cold beer, and a choice selection of (now legal) MJ in our coat pockets. With light hearts and a skip in our steps, we set off together on the short trek up the hill to our favorite happy place—the Arb.

"This is such a blast," said Lloyd.

"I know, but I feel like I'm playing hooky," Mouse confessed.

"Yeah," agreed Kanga, "I've got two papers waiting to be written."

"Come on, you guys," laughed Roach, "we all need a little fun now and then."

"For sure," was the silent consensus, as we eagerly stepped through the heavy iron gates of the arboretum and were instantly enveloped by the mystical winter wonderland awaiting us. In one unspoken accord, we all ran head-long out across the crusty snowfall and up to our favorite (usually grassy) hilltop hangout. Caught in a momentary pause of wonder concerning the wisdom of our course, we courageously pressed on in unison, running and skipping and tumbling down the far side of the hill with childlike whoops and hollers of delight.

As we laughed and danced and sang our way down the snow-covered slope, I began to perceive the glorious scene unfolding in slow motion. Time itself had become a mere idea, as I carefully studied and savored the never-ending moment. The periodic sounds and voices of my beloved friends gently faded away as my inner world came more clearly into focus. A momentary glimpse of my friends walking far off in the distance created a small ripple of fear in my chest. No problem, I thought, I'll just catch up with them later. I know my way around the Arb.

I pulled myself up and out of the snowbank in which I sat and headed off through the woods in search of my friends and entrance gates. As I made my way along, the sun silently slipped below the horizon, the woods grew dark, and at each bend I seemed to lose my bearings and found myself back where I'd begun.

Am I lost? I wondered, with a tinge of panic. Why did they leave me? It's getting so dark. How am I going to find my way out of here? As these nagging thoughts drifted in and out of my mind, I began experiencing a profound sense of connection to everything around me. There were no words or questions or doubts. Only a loving, abiding, all-encompassing sense of peace beyond time and place. I knew I was to look up, and above me, I saw a single point of light. Like a brilliant star hung in the sky, I followed it up and through the shadowy forest and back up the hill to the entrance gates.

My mind continued to rest in a supremely calm, focused, and energized state as I grew increasingly aware of my connection to everything around me. My consciousness expanded to include the entire environment in my span of vision. It was less a thought, and more an awareness or kind of knowing, as the apparent separation between myself and everything else dissolved, and there was only me…or rather, my consciousness. I watched the cars passing along the street, and as the scene gently slowed to a standstill, I noticed how it was all beautifully synchronized with my breathing. For a millisecond, a familiar query broke through the profound silence, peace, and knowing: "Who am I, really?" For days afterward, I contemplated my on-going inner experiences and sensed they were subtly weaving the threads of my life together with every person and thing and showing me—with increasing clarity—we are far more than I had previously imagined.

In addition to my schoolwork, I eased myself into being more outspoken on campus and in surrounding communities and began doing more public speaking. As I grew more comfortable speaking out against the war, racism, and other unjust circumstances in the world, I made a personal commitment to seek out a way to live my life based on the values of unity, acceptance, equality, and spiritual awareness. This, I knew in my bones, was the only authentic way forward for me, and I steadily grew more focused and determined to find and walk a path based on these values. But, I wondered, what would that even look like?

"Hey, Larry, wait up," I heard a familiar voice yell from the sidewalk behind me.

"Hey, Lenny, how ya' doing?" I asked, turning around, and offering my hand. "And what are you up to this fine, frosty morning?"

Lenny was a cool and very creative dude I'd met in one of my RC classes. We really enjoyed hanging out together, and he'd become a close friend. We were both in tune with living and sharing our lives with others in a more intentional kind of way.

"Nothing much, I just got out of class," he said, pulling his trademark cap down over his ears with a little tug. "I'm glad I saw you. You got a minute?"

"Sure, Lenny, what's up?"

"Well, I've got this idea I want to run by you," he said, looking sideways, grinning.

"Okay, I'm listening," I said, with genuine curiosity.

"So, I'm organizing a bunch of guys so we can rent a house together. It's that big, old, brick mansion with the giant front porch, on the next corner up from East Quad. So, it's an easy move," he said, nonchalantly. "And it's a pretty diverse group."

Lenny was of Jewish ancestry combined with a strong and very visible Native American background. His skin was a soft-brown complexion, and his absolutely straight hair was jet black, and he wore it down to the middle of his back.

Lenny and I had spoken together often about the importance of bringing people together and creating a safe space to go beyond our differences and focus on the common good in one another. I sensed this was a big part of what he was up to, and he knew I'd be open to it.

"One guy's in Liberal Arts," he continued, holding up his left thumb. His four fingers shot up as he rattled off, "then there's a med student, a business major, a music major, and there's one other guy that's in the RC with us.

"Plus me," he added, holding up his right thumb. "Plus you," he said, with a gleam in his eye, as he extended his right index finger directly at me, "I'm hoping."

"Sounds like a really interesting mix of people and interests," I said.

"Yeah, they really are. And I know you'll fit right in and love it too. What do you think? I know each of them, and they're all pretty chill guys and open-minded, too."

"Well," I said, "I wasn't really thinking about moving out of East Quad, but it sounds kinda cool."

I was hesitant but, I thought to myself, it really does seem to fit with my interest in living in a more diverse and conscious kind of way. It might be really good.

"We're meeting tomorrow after classes," he said, blowing into his cupped hands and thrusting them back into his coat pockets. "Come on by, and I'll introduce you to everybody. It'll be cool, you'll see."

I accepted Lenny's warm invitation and was pleasantly surprised by how thoroughly I enjoyed meeting everyone the following afternoon. By the end of our time together, we'd all agreed to move in together by the beginning of the next semester. We also agreed to view this new arrangement as an intriguing, most likely challenging, and hopefully enjoyable opportunity to get to know each other, and in the process, expand our understanding of and appreciation for creative living approaches.

Within weeks, we happily found ourselves sitting around the fireplace together in our new living room, watching the sparks weave their way up the flue and soaking in the warmth of the dancing flames.

"Oh, wow," Lenny exclaimed, to everyone's astonishment, as he stood upright. In the glow of the firelight, his dark skin and long, flowing, black hair formed a remarkable likeness to the shaman of some ancient tribe.

"What?" we all pleaded in startled unison.

"This is *just* like that book I loved when I was a kid. I'm sure you guys know it."

We looked around to see if anyone had a clue what he was talking about.

"What was it?—Oh yeah. *The House at Pooh Corner!*" he crowed with glee, as his face blossomed into a broad smile. It was as much a deep pronunciation as it was a treasured recollection, and we soon discovered our common appreciation for the playful adventures of Christopher Robin and his lovable animal friends. "That's it." We agreed we'd call our new home "The House at Pooh Corner." And much like Winnie the Pooh and his quirky companions, we turned our efforts toward the conscious practice of living in a peaceful, mutually supportive way, with the sincere desire to never forget the simple importance of our friendships with one another.

I went grocery shopping one afternoon and feeling creative, decided to cook a big dinner for everyone in the house. Though some were hesitant to try my vegetarian cooking for the first time, everyone came back for seconds.

"This is delicious!" Lenny said. "Where'd you learn to cook like this?"

"Oh, here and there," I answered slyly. Their happy faces made me glad I'd endured all those years of training in Dad's kitchens.

"Hey, I've got an idea," someone suggested, "let's take turns cooking and cleaning up? Then, each of us only has to cook one night a week! What d'ya think?"

There was unanimous agreement, and with a cheer, and another round of brownies, this new arrangement became a regular part of our Pooh Corner tradition.

Sharing our lives in this way was an amazing and uplifting experience. Despite our various outward differences, of which there were many, we felt unified in our common humanity. Much like Professor Mann's classroom experiments, our deliberate practice was to question our assumptions about ourselves and one another. Based on our beliefs and best intentions, our daily lives became the proving ground of our developing convictions, and in the process, we discovered an inherent, loving connection with one another.

In addition to my menagerie of close RC and House at Pooh Corner friends, I was hanging out with an ever-growing crowd of interesting people I met in classes, around campus, and at various political rallies, concerts, and pickup basketball games—including a few U of M basketball team members. With so many new relationships being forged, and my growing interest in political activism, there was never a shortage of places to go, things to do, and people to meet. Ann Arbor, it seemed, was the perfect place for me to be— where it was all happening—and I happily found myself coming alive in the middle of it all.

10

WHEN THE STUDENT IS READY

It was, I realized, all I'd ever been searching for: a pure sensation of freedom, an abiding peace and contentment, and an unexpected and undeniable experience of love and connection rising from within my own heart.

As the semester wound its way down, I was busily completing my undergraduate studies and growing increasingly eager to graduate and get on with whatever the next chapter of my life was going to be. Tea and a chat had become a regular thing.

"Come in, dears," Jean urged, as she ushered me and Dick inside, where we were greeted by the scrumptious aroma of freshly baked bread.

"If you'd be so kind, Larry," she said, turning to me, "please add a log or two and get a nice fire going for us all."

"Gladly," I answered and headed to the living room.

"And you, my dear," she said, turning to Dick with affection, "can go fetch the bread and honey while I put the kettle on."

"Yes, please," Dick agreed, and happily followed her into the kitchen.

"So, Larry," Dick jumped in with his usual enthusiasm, as Jean poured our chai, and we settled into the colorful collection of cushions, "what are your plans after graduation? Are you thinking about grad school?"

"We both think you'd do really well," added Jean quietly, "and enjoy it too."

"It's amazing that you guys are bringing this up," I responded with excitement. "I've been thinking about it a lot lately. I'm really enjoying the teaching and mentoring role I'm playing in your class, Jean. And working with the students has really been a great learning experience for me. I'm realizing that teaching and being part of an educational environment is something I really value and enjoy. I think I might like to pursue it as a career. I feel like I have some valuable life experience I can bring to academics."

"For sure," Jean and Dick said in unison.

"But I'm worried I may not be up to the demands of getting an advanced degree. Plus, I'm more interested in the experience and challenge of learning and teaching than I am in getting more degrees. And it's hard for me to imagine doing grad school in the traditional way."

"Oh, I'm sure we can circumvent that apparent obstacle," Dick offered. "It's certainly not a catastrophe."

"The thing is," I continued, "I also have a really passionate interest in the spiritual part of who I am. I've had some powerful experiences of deeper states of consciousness. and I'm pretty sure they aren't the kind of thing studied in typical psychology programs."

"So, can you tell us more about what's going on for you, Larry?" asked Jean, leaning in with interest.

"Well, I went to church when I was a kid, but I've never really been a religious kind of person like my mom or my sister, Pat. In the army, though, I started having what I'd call "spiritual experiences" and to help figure out what was going on with me, I pretty much read all the books about spirituality that I could find—Western books like *Siddhartha* by Hermann Hesse, and *On the Taboo Against Knowing Who You Are* by Alan Watts, and *Be Here Now* by Ram Dass. Then I started looking for and studying Eastern spiritual writings like the *Upanishads* and was drawn to stories about the sages and masters who experienced higher states of consciousness and who taught their students how to experience these states. I started looking around and found a graduate program in Eastern Psychology at Colorado that looks like it might be right up my alley. So that's what's going on for me."

A gentle silence filled the room as the fire crackled and hissed beside me.

"Well, that's quite interesting, isn't it?" Dick finally said with a chuckle. "Because Jean and I have become increasingly curious and drawn to the spiritual dimension of consciousness ourselves."

"Yes, we have," agreed Jean with smiling eyes and a lightness in her voice, "and we've been learning how to meditate too."

"Well," I said with relief, "I think this is what they call serendipity."

For the next several hours, our conversation was filled with an uplifting sense of liberation and excitement. Each of us had experienced our own form of an awakening to some larger form of reality beyond our day-to-day lives. These experiences had changed us in profound ways and opened a door to a shared understanding of what had, until now, been a semi-secret part of my life—and theirs too.

"For me," I explained, "it's hard to talk about, mostly because it feels so impossible to find the right words to describe such profound experiences."

"Exactly," Dick chimed in. "How can words capture the consciousness at the core of our existence, the universe, and everything in it?"

"Yes," Jean agreed, "words can only approximate the experience."

"It's not like I was looking for all of this either," I said, "at least not consciously. But the truth of what I witnessed is undeniable, even though I struggle to make much logical sense of it."

Our common experiences had, we discovered, opened in each of us an on-going search for meaning. We had more questions than answers but we also shared a common understanding that there was no turning back. We wanted more and were committed to finding it. We were keenly interested in the core of ourselves and others, and we each sensed this, in large part, is what had drawn us to the field of psychology, and now...somehow, beyond.

Somewhere around midnight, we finally said our goodnights, and as I walked back to the House at Pooh Corner, I was struck by how extraordinarily good it was to have a normal, semi-rational conversation about my mystical experiences and not feel judged or weird about it. I recalled what the famous psychologist William James had written about the difficulty of communicating about such experiences: "...No adequate report or explanation of the experience can be given by words." It seemed funny but oddly reassuring to know my beloved and distinguished academic mentors—psychology and sociology professors— were wondering, right along with me, what path to take and where and how to find a teacher, coach, or perhaps a sage to provide guidance and answers along the way.

With two plus years' worth of credits from FDU and another year's worth from Western New England College, I graduated from the University of Michigan at the end of my first year in the RC. Through the connections he'd made in his labor relations work, my friend Mouse found us summer jobs at the Rawsonville Ford factory in Ypsilanti. It was grueling work, but we only worked Fridays, Saturdays, and Sundays and got paid double time, which felt like very big money to us.

Over the summer, I continued meeting with Dick and Jean Mann. As I learned more about the resources, options, and opportunities at Michigan, I came to see how well they matched my interests, and the wisdom of staying in Ann Arbor, for the time being, anyway. Dick calmly guided me through the labyrinth of forms, signatures, transcripts, and a multitude of other requirements, and in a matter of weeks I was enrolled in the Graduate School of Educational Psychology at U of M.

It felt like a big step in the right direction, and I soon discovered that I loved it. I loved the learning process and the whole university environment. I loved the depth and breadth of the course work and the readings, the lectures and seminars, the research, and in particular, I loved the teaching, with all of its challenges. Working alongside Dick and Jean and the graduate school advisor that Dick had introduced me to, I served as a teaching assistant at both the graduate and undergraduate levels. As I gained more confidence, I began to experience teaching as a natural and critical extension of the learning process. I was finding my way, and under the guidance and inspiration of my mentors, I began to envision a career as a college lecturer or maybe even a full professor. My mentors saw this potential in me, and I felt a growing sense of purpose in myself.

"Hey, Larry," Dick said after class one afternoon. "Hold up a minute. Something really great is happening."

"Oh yeah, what's up?" I asked.

"There's a spiritual teacher from India who's coming to Ann Arbor, and we've arranged a special meeting with him —something his folks call a *darshan*. It's for all interested psychology faculty and graduate students. He's considered a meditation master, and given our common interests, I figured you'd want to come."

"Cool. Thanks," I said. "Sounds interesting. I'll catch up with you later."

I had just enough time to get to a meeting with one of my undergraduate students at a downtown coffee shop. On my way there, I walked past a poster in one of the shop windows with a picture of a hip-looking, bearded dude in a big, fuzzy, woolen hat. Maybe he's a jazz musician? I wondered. I like jazz. *BE WITH BABA*, the poster said in large letters. I took a closer look. Huh, I thought, as I read the fine print. He's a guru. Maybe that's what I need? Someone who understands this whole spiritual journey thing better than I do. That would be helpful.

I stopped by the Mann's house after my meeting to get the scoop.

"So, what's up with this Baba guy?" I asked, when Dick answered the door. "I just saw a poster downtown that describes him as a living master of meditation and the inner journey."

"Hey, Larry, come on in," Dick said, walking into the living room and offering me a seat. "Yeah, his name is Swami Muktananda, but apparently his students and followers call him Baba, which is a term of affection and respect, and means father. He's considered a living saint in India and has thousands of followers from all different walks of life. The idea behind this darshan meeting with him is to gain insights from the yoga psychology of the Eastern tradition to add to our Western approach to the mind and psyche. It should be interesting and possibly fascinating. It certainly seems worth looking into, don't you think?"

The meeting was held in an old, rambling, three-story fraternity house. When I opened the heavy front door, I felt an air of anticipation. Forty or fifty people were sitting on the floor, squeezed into the sizable living room and dining room, and even up the stairway to the second floor. The place was packed, so I stood in the back.

One of the Indian men, who looked like he was in charge, stood up and beckoned me with the back of his hand. "Come, my friend," he said pleasantly, bobbing his head from side to side, "there's room for you here."

From where I stood it looked like standing-room-only, but as I inched my way closer, several people slid over and provided a space for me to sit on the floor directly next to the holy man's chair. When he walked in and sat down, I was surprised by the full force of his energy, which until then, I didn't know was even a thing. The waves or vibrations emanating from him made listening to the content of his talk quite difficult, though it was a peaceful and pleasant sensation. He spoke in warm and melodic tones, pausing just long enough for his words to be translated into English. The power of the mind was his primary topic, and how it can cause so much suffering.

"On the other hand," he said, raising his index finger in the air, "if we are able to control and focus our mind properly, it can become our greatest friend. And this, more than our outer circumstances, is the secret to a happy life. So," he concluded, "this is my mission and teaching: that you should add meditation to your life. It is very simple and meant for everyone, and it doesn't go against any religion that you follow. It's just one step deeper than the state of sleep. This is why everyone should meditate, including—or perhaps especially—psychologists," he added with an infectious laugh.

I felt myself slipping in and out of my normal consciousness as a powerful energy focused my thoughts on the deep meaning and implications of his words and the meditative state itself. I was actually spontaneously going in and out of meditation. And in that state, I felt incredibly light and energized, as though the laws of gravity were suspended, and my body was floating just above the floor.

When his talk ended, everyone was invited to come up and be introduced to him. Since I was sitting right next to his seat, I stayed put. He looked down at me and asked his interpreter, "What's his name?"

Before I could respond, Professor Mann introduced me. I felt an intense and inexplicable resonance with this Indian holy man and his simple message that meditation is the way to connect with the inner consciousness.

After the program, as I was walking away from the big, old house, I felt prompted to turn around and look back. Up on the third-floor balcony, the meditation master was standing by himself and facing in my direction. I had the undeniable sense that he'd been looking directly at me and had gently tapped me on the shoulder to make sure I got the point: "*If you didn't get the message from my talk, get it now.*" A powerful but peaceful energy was emanating from him, causing a sympathetic feeling deep inside me. Like a spiritual tuning fork, I recognized at once this was the same deep resonance I'd been awakened to and was continuing to seek. Forget all the fancy words in the ancient scriptures and philosophical texts I'd been reading so voraciously. This was beyond any words. It was, I realized, all I'd ever been searching for: an exquisitely pure sensation of freedom, an abiding peace and contentment, and an unexpected and undeniable experience of love and connection rising from within my own heart.

I heard about an intensive meditation workshop being taught by the holy man down in Ohio, and I attended a few weeks later with my friend Lloyd and his girlfriend, Barbara. It was a very focused, intense experience of learning meditation over a long weekend. We spent several days around the Indian sage listening to him talk in greater depth about the importance of meditation on the spiritual path. During our times of meditation, some of which were as long as an hour, my mind became very calm and peaceful, and I caught more glimpses of the inner state I'd experienced when he was standing on the balcony back in Ann Arbor.

"Yoga happens when the mind becomes quiet and still," he said after one particularly memorable meditation session. "This takes practice, and the awakening of spiritual energy is the key," he added after a long pause. "Meditation is the main means of practice."

Another light bulb went off inside of me. My experience in the army must have been a kind of spiritual awakening, and meditation will help me consolidate and integrate it into my life. That's why he keeps stressing its importance.

At the end of the weekend workshop, when I came up to say goodbye, he looked very warm and beamed with joy. Then he looked at me quite sternly and through his interpreter, said,

"Study. Do your work. Go to the ashram, and don't be a nuisance."

What? Why did he say that? Maybe it was like one of those Zen koans that nobody understands: What is the sound of one hand clapping? His stern directive felt deeply personal and oddly important. It reminded me of when my dad was training me in the kitchen. I felt a bit hurt, at first. My mind and ego argued that he didn't know me at all, so how could he say such a thing. But his words stayed with me, sinking in, and unraveling in my deeper awareness.

"What did he say to you when we were leaving?" Lloyd asked, on our drive back to Ann Arbor. "Something about being a nuisance?" he asked with a giggle.

"Yeah, it was," I said sheepishly. "He told me to go to the ashram and do my work, and not be a nuisance."

"What does that mean?" Lloyd asked.

"I'm not quite sure," I said, "but I think maybe he was reminding me to meditate—at a center or at work, or wherever—to stay in touch with my inner Self more often."

"Okay," he said, sitting up in his seat. "But what does that have to do with not being a nuisance?"

"Who knows? Maybe he was telling me the same thing Rob, my professor back at Western New England College told me, that I don't have to call myself a radical, or be a nuisance, or anything else, for that matter. I just need to be myself, and let others do the same."

"Right on," agreed Lloyd with a smile.

Back in Ann Arbor, I began meditating and chanting regularly each morning before starting my busy days of graduate studies and teaching. Within weeks, I felt the focus and quality of my thought processes gaining greater depth, clarity, and compassion. Meeting this unassuming holy man from India felt like the next big step in the unfolding of my life, as though I was standing on the threshold of an exciting new adventure. I'd only spent a few hours with him but somehow felt awakened to a profound transformation in my personal, academic, and spiritual life, and began to see how each part of my life was connected.

The director in charge of the meditation center in Ann Arbor mentioned that Baba had moved into an old hotel in Oakland, California, and was in the process of turning it into a meditation center. It was getting near the end of the school year, and my summer plans were still up in the air. If I could experience such positive changes in my life by just spending a couple of days with this meditation master, I wondered what spending the summer with him might bring my way.

"It's a great opportunity," the ashram director suggested, when I asked about the possibility. "You could spend some quality time with Baba out in Oakland and see where it takes you."

What would it be like to live in a yoga ashram with a holy man? I wondered. And what is a holy man, anyway? Will he be able to help me integrate all my spiritual experiences with my day-to-day life as a graduate student? And how can all this be woven into the career path that appears to be opening up for me?

I figured there was only one way to find out, and promptly started planning my long drive to California in the trusty Mustang.

It hadn't really occurred to me that getting on with my life in this way would include yet another unexpected, life-defining, and exciting step into the unknown. Or that this particular trip west would end up taking me so far east—to India—and well beyond. I couldn't have known how this next leg of the journey would ultimately change the entire trajectory and purpose of my life.

But I'm getting ahead of myself here. That's the subject for another book.

FULL CIRCLE

AFTERWORD

There have been numerous iterations of this book, starting in the early 1990s. This particular version began in 2014 as a rather sizable collection of stories from a long series of regular conversations in a favorite cafe in Melbourne, Australia. Each week my dear friend, the writer Meme McDonald, and I ordered our coffees and found a comfortable place to sit. She then proceeded to ask me a seemingly endless set of questions and promptly type my responses into her computer—at lightning speed!

"Where do you think all this is taking us?" I asked her after several months, feeling a bit impatient with the whole process. She looked a bit puzzled. "It's just that I was imagining," I continued, "you were going to be coaching me to write about my experiences as a monk, and my professional approach to leadership and personal development. When do we get to all that?" She gazed calmly over the top of her reading glasses with a bemused lift of her eyebrows and responded with a question of her own.

"Are any of the approaches you take in your conscious leadership and life purpose coaching work around the world based on your experiences and learnings growing up?"

"Well," I answered, catching a glimmer of where she was headed, "for sure."

"Well then," she said with a chuckle, "your approach is the result and reflection of what you've been taught, lived through, and learned along the way. That's the starting point. To truly understand why you do what you do, and how you do it, people need to understand you and what your life story has exposed you to and taught you.

Everything else you've done comes later." I just sat there with my mouth open. She was spot on.

There's immense value in looking backwards at our life journey in a focused, intentional way. It helps us to feel the heart of our experiences more deeply and to clarify the meaning and significance they hold for us. Mining our stories enables us to find and follow the hidden threads, identify patterns, make connections, and integrate the seemingly disjointed or conflicting elements of our journey. Ultimately, it allows us to uncover a broader set of possibilities, and a clearer sense of purpose for our lives moving forward.

With this book completed, we're eager to keep going. So, stay tuned, and please let us know how these stories have touched you (LarryHolmesPracticalWisdom.com). We hope they've shed a bit of light on your path and inspired you to dig a little deeper and sift through the stories of your own, unique life journey. Please consider using the reflection questions below to help you begin to re-frame the past in new ways. May you find valuable insights to free you from limiting thought patterns and behaviors, and to help you to live life more fully, with heart and purpose.

Be The Light

Be well and have a good life, my friend.

With all good graces, may you find the peace and love you seek and so richly deserve.

Let the beauty within your being shine forth on the outside, so that all may see you as you truly are.

Understand that whatever doubt you may have is the product of a confused mind, which is something you can overcome.

Focus on the strength of your heart and soul.

Find your passion and purpose in this world, whatever that may be, and live true to yourself, in a way that allows you to be true to others as well.

And above all, know that the inner light is real, and with you always. It is the love you experience in your own heart.

Remember this—whatever missteps you make or think you make, be compassionate and forgiving.

You are light to all. Be that light.

1. Larry shares many of his parents' beliefs and cultural opinions, and their favorite ways of expressing them. These "mantras" about what makes sense in the world, and what doesn't, frame much of his early childhood memories and impact many of his future decisions, for better or worse.

   a. What "mantras" from your early childhood do you remember hearing?

   b. Did they resonate with you, or did you feel a tug in another direction?

   c. Have you hung onto any of these frameworks into adulthood?

   d. How have they shaped your decision making so far in life?

2. During his transition into high school, Larry says that "nothing felt familiar or easy. That much change, and that quickly, wasn't easy." He was no longer part of the racial majority. His classmates made assumptions about his academic goals. One teacher doubted his capabilities. He started playing basketball at a much higher level.

   a. What major life transitions did you experience during adolescence?

   b. How did they impact your journey into adulthood?

   c. How do your narratives about those times of change influence you now?

3. Throughout the book, Larry reflects on the words of his mentor in high school, Henry Moore: "Who you listen to

is important. Everyone has an opinion. What matters is who comes to you with light. People who offer you love and support and wisdom. Those are the people to listen to." This lesson of finding the light took many forms for Larry, but a common theme was meeting a person who encouraged or demonstrated an openness and genuine interest in following what is uplifting, positive, and productive.

    a. What times in your life did you feel surrounded by and stuck in negativity?

    b. Who helped you, even in difficult situations, to find the positive possibilities?

    c. What did you have to let go of in order to move forward?

    d. What did you gain?

4. The tensions between Larry and his dad, and Larry's ongoing struggles to push back against his dad's expectations show up repeatedly throughout these stories.

    a. When, during your adolescence or early adulthood, did you ignore your instincts and/or compromise your inner beliefs or notions in favor of someone else's?

    b. What were the consequences?

    c. Why, at the time, was it so hard for you to distinguish between internal and external influences when making decisions?

    d. How has that changed over time?

5. After making the decision to reduce his class load, Larry's life was drastically upended when he was drafted into the army.

    a. When have seemingly inconsequential decisions you made led to unforeseen, life-changing, or perhaps even devastating events or consequences?

    b. How did this impact your life?

    c. What did you learn about yourself?

6. After standing up for his fellow Trainee, who was face down in the snow, Larry's drill sergeant remarks, "You may have been surprised to find you have some form of courage in yourself, am I right?"

    a. When have you been surprised by courage in yourself?

    b. How did that courage manifest?

    c. Why? What prompted you to find it?

7. Larry was tempted to paint his time in the army with a broad brush of negativity. But over time he began to see how much he was learning about himself, life, and leadership, through the experience.

    a. What key moments or periods in your life do you tend to summarize negatively?

    b. What deeper lessons or wisdom do these challenging experiences hold for you?

   c. What would it be like to hold both kinds of feelings at the same time?

8. "Who am I? Where am I going? What is my purpose?" These are the pressing questions Larry asks himself repeatedly throughout these stories.

   a. Have you been able to answer any of these questions for yourself?

   b. What kinds of conclusions have you come to?

   c. If these are new questions for you, what would help you answer them?

9. In chapter 9, Larry makes a commitment to live his life "based on the values of unity, acceptance, equality, and spiritual awareness." He goes on to say, "This, I knew in my bones, was the only authentic way forward for me, and I steadily grew more focused and determined to find and walk a path based on these values."

   a. What are some of the core values that inform your decision making as an adult?

   b. How have they changed throughout your life?

   c. Which of these values were passed down to you?

   d. Which did you discover "in your bones," through personal reflection or deep inner experiences?

ACKNOWLEDGEMENTS

My heartfelt gratitude goes to Meme McDonald for teaching me the deeper purpose and meaning of stories, and to Paul Kron for coming alongside to help me plow the ground, plant the seeds, harvest and grind the grain, and bake the bread.

To my spiritual guide, Baba Muktananda, and to my academic mentor and friend, Dick Mann, I offer my sincere love, respect, and gratitude.

To Henry Moore, and my many other mentors, teachers, coaches (Vinnie Ernst), and friends (Stan, Roach, Mouse, Kanga)—mentioned (or not) in this book—who were there for me and offered the light when I most needed it, to each of you I offer my love and sincere thanks.

Much gratitude goes to Laura Duggan, our kind and relentless editor at Nicasio Press, for your wisdom and patience in getting us to the finish line. And to our first readers, Ruth Morton and Katie Kron, for your fresh points of view, deep insights, difficult questions, and helpful suggestions.

My deep thanks go to my wife, Louanne, and children, Chloe and Summer, for loving me and enduring my notions of writing a book these past few decades. And to Al Jr., Pat, Ralph, Bruce, and Victor for your loving support of me on the unusual paths I've taken.

Loving thanks and gratitude to my dear nephew, Cooper James, for believing in me and my story, and encouraging me to write this book about my circuitous journey.

I also received timely encouragement from Jim Shomos.

A special thank you to everyone who contributed to my fundraising campaign, for your generous support and encouragement during these past few years of writing.

And one final, but sincere thank you to you, the reader, for bringing these tales full circle, by reading them.

FULL CIRCLE

ABOUT THE AUTHOR

Larry Holmes is a compelling facilitator in the realm of "Life Purpose Coaching"—a transformative, one-on-one journey designed for those hungry to unearth and find clarity in their authentic path and purpose in life. Larry's forte lies in empathetically guiding individuals through the personal cultivation of a conscious lifestyle leveraging their innate talents and gifts.

Spanning an international career as a corporate consultant, mentor, and confidante to people across business, government, education, sports, and the arts, Larry boasts nearly four decades of expertise in organizational change, learning, leadership, and individual and team development.

Larry's academic roots trace back to the University of Michigan, where his studies embraced a multifaceted approach, ranging from group dynamics, sociology, and urban studies to educational and developmental psychology.

His prowess as a presenter, facilitator, and educator has been acknowledged at various institutions, including Harvard University, Princeton University, the University of California, the All-India Institute of Medical Sciences, and the Australian Academy of Sciences.

Through his overarching theme of "Practical Wisdom," Larry has dedicated his efforts to orchestrating highly effective change management within organizations, placing a premium on leadership and teamwork development.

Larry's passions also extend into sports psychology and peak performance coaching. As a former college basketball player, he has crafted "Mind Sports"—a unique developmental system designed to assist professional sports teams and individuals in achieving new heights.

Larry is known for his uncanny ability to distill profound and intricate concepts into crystal-clear insights. His engaging and humorous approach to storytelling invites us to mine our own unique life stories and embark on a transformative odyssey where purpose meets practical wisdom and resonates with meaning.

Paul Kron has been an environmental design and community planning consultant for over forty years. For two of those decades he also served as Adjunct Professor of Landscape Architecture at North Carolina A&T State University. As one who has benefited greatly from Larry's wise and loving counsel since Ann Arbor days in the early 1970s, Paul jumped at the chance to work on this project with his beloved friend and mentor. Yes, for the joy of hanging out with him more regularly. But especially for the privilege of helping Larry share his heartfelt, practical wisdom with others.

www.ingramcontent.com/pod-product-compliance
Lightning Source LLC
Chambersburg PA
CBHW060803120626

46557CB00001B/67